P9-AOZ-285

Borders
& Bridges

Borders
& Bridges

Mennonite Witness
in a Religiously Diverse World

Edited by
**Peter Dula and
Alain Epp Weaver**

Foreword by
Stanley W. Green

Cascadia

Publishing House
Telford, Pennsylvania

copublished with
Herald Press
Scottdale, Pennsylvania

Cascadia Publishing House LLC orders, information, reprint permissions:
contact@cascadiapublishinghouse.com
1-215-723-9125
126 Klingerman Road, Telford PA 18969
www.CascadiaPublishingHouse.com

Borders and Bridges
Copyright © 2007 by Cascadia Publishing House
a division of Cascadia Publishing House LLC, Telford, PA 18969
All rights reserved.
Copublished with Herald Press, Scottdale, PA
Library of Congress Catalog Number: 2007027236
ISBN 13: 978-1-931038-46-1; **ISBN 10:** 1-931038-46-5
Book design by Cascadia Publishing House
Cover design by Merrill R. Miller

The paper used in this publication is recycled and meets the
minimum requirements of American National Standard for Information Sciences—Permanence of Paper for Printed Library Materials,
ANSI Z39.48-1984.

All Bible quotations are used by permission, all rights reserved and,
unless otherwise noted, are from *The New Revised Standard Version of
the Bible*, copyright 1989, by the Division of Christian Education of the
National Council of the Churches of Christ in the USA.

Library of Congress Cataloguing-in-Publication Data

Borders and bridges : Mennonite witness in a religiously diverse
world / edited by Alain Epp Weaver and Peter Dula ; foreword by
Stanley Green.
    p. cm.
Includes bibliographical references and index.
ISBN-13: 978-1-931038-46-1 (trade pbk. : alk. paper)
ISBN-10: 1-931038-46-5 (trade pbk. : alk. paper)
1. Peace--Religious aspects--Mennonites--Case studies. I. Weaver,
Alain Epp. II. Dula, Peter, 1970-
BX8128.P4B67 2007
289.7--dc22

                    2007027236

        15 13 12 11 10 09 08 07   10 9 8 7 6 5 4 3 2 1

Contents

Foreword

*D*ialogical conversations or theological debates have their value. In the accounts that follow, however, entering into authentic human relationships across boundaries of geography, culture, religion, and language is seen as foundational for sharing the good news of Jesus. The encounters are shaped by the particularities of each context. The stories are different. Yet all have in common a commitment to non-coercive human engagement that values the other. Robert Wuthnow observes that

> At no time in its history has the Judeo-Christian tradition been able to confine its interests within narrow . . . boundaries. The Hebrew Scriptures tell of a people forced to migrate beyond their own borders in search of food, displacing local gods with a God of the heavens, and recurrently finding themselves caught in the intrigues of warring empires. Jesus constantly ran into the limiting presuppositions of such boundaries in his day, and he repeatedly cut through them to enlarge his followers' vision. . . .[1]

Engagement with the world beyond requires movement and anticipates transformation. Jesus himself was constantly on the move. Along the way, he crossed many boundaries and engaged the people of the borderlands. It is no accident that Jesus envisions his disciples crossing borders to "Jerusalem, all of Judea and Samaria, and to the ends of the earth" (Acts 1:8).

A lack of engagement beyond ourselves and our communities presumes stasis. Stasis ultimately leads to death. Entering into relationship presumes movement. Robert Wuthnow in *Sharing the Journey*[2] alludes to the dual sociology in flourishing congregations of "joining" and "belonging." Joining is predicated on the porosity of boundaries. It stimulates passion, energy, vision, creativity and movement. Belonging, on the other hand, engenders clarity, roots, and connectedness.

Boundaries are important. They help us to know who we are and where we come from. For missional communities, however, crossing borders is essential. A church with a missional consciousness understands that boundaries are not exclusive. Differences are important but enrich community. This is the good news according to the gospel: God is creating a new humanity.

But it is not a generic humanity. This new peoplehood is constituted by people from different ethnicities, languages, cultures. This is the mystery now made known: In the church, comprised of many cultures and ethnicities, Gods' purposes are being revealed (Eph. 3:3-6). For the people of God, borders are identifiers of communities incorporated in God's design with whom we are to be engaged for God's sake. Our differences are important not as tools for exclusion but as the measure of our diversity and completion. Openness to diversity enables a greater appreciation of the richness our differences make possible.

A tragic mistake in mission has been objectifying people through a "results" orientation that turns converts into data for showcasing our efficient methods or sincere dedication. In this mindset, relationships were instrumental; stereotypes, if not encouraged, were left intact. The focus was on teaching rather than on learning. As the stories of interfaith-bridge-building reported in this text show, engagements built on developing authentic relationships can be subversive. They force us to question and ultimately invalidate stereotypes. An Anabaptist commitment to a non-coercive posture vis-à-vis others gives us the freedom to be authentic. We can share our story freely in a way that is respectful and preserves the dignity of others rather than making them targets or data in an outcomes-based strategy.

Not always blatantly stated in the accounts but often implied is a response to the question, Why should we cross borders and build bridges? Andrew Walls, commenting on God's purpose in gathering "a numberless multitude drawn from every tribe, tongue, people and nation" (Rev. 7:9), observes that this is not simply a fulfillment God's design but a necessary expression of our completion. We are inadequate until people from across every border are welcomed into God's family. Walls says,

Paul speaks of Jews and Gentiles growing together, and he says that only when the two strands are one will they have grown into the full stature of Christ. . . .

We live now at a time when the church is multicultural. I think that the fullness of . . . Christ will emerge only when Christians from all these cultures come together. If I understand what Paul says in Ephesians correctly, it is as though Christ himself is growing as the different cultures are brought together in him.[3]

The accounts in this book encourage a new way of thinking about how we witness to the good news. As we share our story in the context of authentic relationships, we are liberated from a savior syndrome. We are freed to enter into new relationships with people everywhere supported by the conviction that we have come to learn, to be enriched, indeed to be completed.

In that space of engagement, we must still fully share our own narrative. For Anabaptists that narrative includes the Bible, centered on Jesus, the gift of God for the salvation of the world and the One in whom all things hold together (Eph. 1:17-23). The story also includes the centuries of commitment to reconciliation and peacemaking. If such sharing attracts others to incorporate this story as part of their narrative, then we must celebrate this as the work of God who effects conversion by the Holy Spirit. As Anabaptists it would be disingenuous and antithetical to the core of our identity to deny this possibility.

Whether through the vissicitudes of history or intentional theological choice, Anabaptists have embraced a pilgrim identity. For pilgrim people, borders and building bridges are part of the fabric of life. This book's stories and reflections inspire us to be pilgrims with a purpose: God's.

—*Stanley W. Green, Goshen, Indiana*
Executive Director, Mennonite Mission Network

NOTES

1. *Rediscovering the Sacred: Perspectives on Religion in Contemporary Society* (Grand Rapids: William B. Eerdmans, 1992), p. 153.

2. *Sharing the Journey* (New York: Free Press, 1994), p. 341-366.

3. "The Expansion of Christianity: An Interview with Andrew Walls ,"*The Christian Century* (Aug. 2-9, 2000), 792- 799.

Acknowledgments

We would like to thank Bob Herr and Judy Zimmerman Herr of Mennonite Central Committee's Peace Office for their unflagging encouragement and support of this project from the beginning. Jan Janzen and Rick Janzen of MCC's Europe and Middle East department also provided invaluable counsel and assistance. Thanks to Ardell Stauffer, who compiled the index. Finally, we wish to thank members of MCC's Peace Committee who first offered feedback on initial versions of portions of this volume at a March 2004 meeting in Akron, Pennsylvania.

—*Alain Epp Weaver*
   Chicago, Illinois; and
   Peter Dula
   Harrisonburg, Virginia

Introduction: Meeting Jesus in the Borderlands

Alain Epp Weaver

*T*ime and again in Scripture, Jesus meets us in the borderlands. At geographical borders and at the divides of faith and ethnicity, Jesus reveals himself and the nature of God's reign to us. The Spirit of God descended upon Jesus and the Father proclaimed his pleasure with the Son as Jesus received his baptism from John in the waters of that ancient dividing river, the border into the land of promise, the Jordan (Matt. 3:13-17). In conversation with a woman of "ill-repute," to use the archaic and delicate phrase, a woman on the fringes of her society, a *Samaritan* woman, no less, a member of a religious group whom self-respecting Jews would have viewed with suspicion at best, Jesus proclaims himself the water of life (John 4:1-26).

An encounter with a Samaritan proves decisive again in Jesus' parable of the traveler headed down to Jericho attacked by bandits and left by the side of the road: By identifying the Samaritan who stops to tend to the injured man as "neighbor," Jesus tells his listeners of the boundary-breaking character of God's coming, even-now-present, reign (Luke 10:25-37). And it is after crossing north into the region of Tyre, today in war-ravaged southern Lebanon, that Jesus meets the unnamed Syrophoenician woman desperate for Jesus to heal her demon-possessed daughter. Through Jesus' conversation with this persistent and faith-filled woman, the overflowing expansiveness of the new reality Jesus has come to proclaim and embody becomes clear (Mark 7:24-30).

Borderlands, as Scripture shows, are often sites of revelation. In today's world, as in the world of the Bible, borderlands are also often sites of tension, clash, even violence. These borderlands can be physical regions separating different political and geographical territories, but just as often they are metaphorical divides, divides between different ethnicities, different socioeconomic classes, and different faiths. Tensions simmer along these borders and sometimes erupt with violent results.

Some political commentators today proclaim that the world is facing a "clash of civilizations," with conflicts brewing and breaking out along religious divides. For these pundits, the events of September 11, 2001, serve as proof positive of a civilizational clash between the West and the Muslim world. Extremist Islamist groups such as Al-Qa'eda, meanwhile, return the favor, portraying U.S.-led invasions of Afghanistan and Iraq as new crusades waged by the supposedly Christian West against the Muslim *ummah.*

If, however, the "clash of civilizations" thesis has rhetorical power, an ability to mobilize people for anticipated battle, it fails to capture the complexities of the real world. Cultures and civilizations are not monolithic, homogenous entities. The dividing lines between ethnic groups, religions, and cultures are always fluid, never fixed. Proponents of battle live alongside persons who seek to build bridges of friendship and cooperation across perceived dividing lines. If religious rhetoric and ideologies are routinely marshalled to justify violence and aggression against the religious "Other," religious texts and traditions also regularly provide visions of peace, justice, and co-existence with the Other.

This volume of essays offers case studies of persons and institutions building bridges across religious divides, of people of different faith backgrounds meeting Jesus in the borderlands. These case studies all emerge out of the worldwide experience of Mennonite Central Committee (MCC), a relief, development, and peacebuilding agency of Mennonite and Brethren in Christ churches in Canada and the United States. MCC recently (see

Appendix) identified "interfaith bridge building"—supporting interfaith collaboration in diaconal ministries of relief, community development, and peacebuilding—as a global "key initiative" for its peacebuilding work. This book is a product of the conviction that if MCC—and other Mennonite institutions, be they mission agencies or conflict transformation institutes—wishes to engage in interfaith bridge building, it is important to learn from the rich Mennonite history of promoting interfaith and ecumenical cooperation.

The authors of the case studies, all of whom have extensive experience with MCC, examine MCC-supported efforts to foster collaboration across religious divides in contexts ranging from Indonesia to Palestine-Israel, from El Salvador to India, and from Nigeria to Nepal. Most of these case studies explore examples of interfaith bridge building—between Christians and Muslims, Christians and Hindus—but others also address the matter of bridging ecumenical rifts, whether between Catholics and evangelicals in Central America or among Protestant, Catholic, and Orthodox Christians in the countries emerging from the break-up of the former Yugoslavia. Many of the case studies, moreover, stress how MCC, as a North American Christian organization, has sought to engage in interfaith collaboration in partnership with local churches, be it with the Mennonite churches of Indonesia or the Coptic Orthodox and Syrian Orthodox churches of the Middle East.

Mennonite Central Committee, a North American Christian organization working in over fifty countries, is a complex institution, and the case studies shed light on some of that complexity. MCC is an organization supported by and accountable to Canadian and U.S. churches, yet it also views itself as accountable in some way to partner organizations and bodies, including especially church and church-related institutions, in the varied contexts where it works. It is an organization staffed not only by "service workers"—the successor term to the now-outmoded "volunteers"—but also by locally hired workers.

MCC speaks much of the same language as the rest of the world of humanitarian non-governmental organizations (NGOs), be they religious like World Vision or secular like Mercy Corps, but in other ways MCC bears striking similarities to the world of mission agencies; indeed, in certain contexts MCC works in close cooperation with Mennonite mission boards. A variety of factors, then—MCC's relationship to the churches in a given country, connections with other Mennonite agencies, feedback from supporting churches in Canada and the United States, and the individual personalities and convictions of MCC workers—all contribute to the shape that MCC's interfaith and ecumenical bridge-building efforts take in different contexts.

At its best, interfaith bridge building is a form of Christian witness and mission. As Peter Dula explains in his concluding essay, Christians have strong christological reasons for attending closely to the voices of those who are *extra muros ecclesiae* (outside the walls of the church). Interfaith bridge building is not about adherents of different faiths relinquishing their truth claims, about finding a supposedly neutral space free of confessional bias, or about watering down religious convictions to a lowest common denominator. For Christians, interfaith bridge building is motivated by the confession that Jesus Christ is Lord over all of creation and history. Thus we should expect to meet Jesus in the borderlands, in our interactions with persons of other faiths.

Cultivating an open receptivity to hearing Jesus' voice in these encounters and building bridges of practical interfaith collaboration in relief, development, and peacebuilding ventures are thus vital forms of Christian witness. We offer these case studies with the hope and the prayer that the church might continue to explore new and creative interfaith collaborations and thus be ready to meet Jesus in the borderlands.

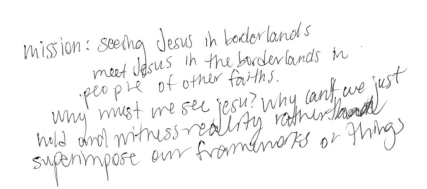

mission: seeing Jesus in borderlands
meet Jesus in the borderlands in
people of other faiths.
why must we see Jesu? why cant we just
hold and witness reality rather than
superimpose our frameworks or things)

Borders
& Bridges

Chapter 1

Indonesia: Living in the Mystery

Jeanne Zimmerly Jantzi

A STORY OF TRANSFORMATION

Usually a bridge is built out from the edges to meet in the middle. This is a story of a bridge that began the other way around. It began with some Indonesian Christians and Indonesian Muslims as well as people of other faiths who were open to working together for the good of their city. Both groups used their networks of personal relationships to build an ever widening circle of trust. From the relationships developed between moderate Indonesian Muslims and Christians emerge new and surprising possibilities of connection, relationship, and reconciliation. Friendships develop even between hardline Muslims—who have hated Westerners and Christians—and Christians from the United States, whose government is perceived by many Muslims, including Indonesian Muslims, as waging a crusade against Islam.

In October 2001, in the days leading up to the U.S. invasion of Afghanistan, many Indonesian Muslims perceived the U.S. actions as a religious attack on Islam. Hardline Muslim groups in Central Java threatened to sweep all Americans out of Solo and the surrounding area. Agus Hariyanto (name changed), the commander of a militant group in Solo, Central Java, took the lead among hardline groups to carry out the sweeping. Political cartoons at the time portrayed this battalion and other radical Islamic groups sweeping the "dirt" out of Central Java with a broom.

The hardliners threatened to remove Americans from hotels and homes and demanded that they immediately leave the country. The U.S. government and other Western nations advised their citizens to leave Indonesia. Embassies sent all non-essential personnel home.

Our family lives in the city of Salatiga in Central Java, where there is a small international mission school. In October 2001, in response to the sweeping threat and two bomb threats in one day at the mission school, many international mission agencies and sending churches connected with the school demanded that their expatriate personnel leave Central Java. Mennonite Central Committee may have been the only organization that allowed those of us living in the situation, rather than administrators in North American headquarters, to make our own decision about whether or not to stay amid the threat. In a matter of three October days, the number of Americans living in Salatiga rapidly dwindled from ninety-five people to our family of five. During that time, a Muslim neighbor family in Salatiga offered to hide us in their home if things got really bad for Americans.

At the same time that Agus was fomenting anti-Americanism, Mennonite and interfaith leader Paulus Hartono was working at community organizing with moderate Muslims and other member groups of the Forum for Peace Across Religions and Groups (FPLAG). In response to the tensions, the interfaith group mapped the city of Solo and developed a telephone network through which leaders of different faiths could warn their counterparts of unrest and work to bring calm. Eventually the tensions lessened and the situation stabilized. By January 2002, many expatriates had returned to Indonesia.

Religious conflict continued to erupt in areas such as Poso in Central Sulawesi and in the Moluccas. Local people there reported that people from other islands incited the violence. Thousands of Christians and Muslims were killed in more than two years of fighting. In 2002, Agus led his battalion far from Central

Java to fight in Ambon in the Moluccas. During the years of conflict, fifty of Agus's Muslim soldiers were killed in combat in Ambon and Poso.

In spring 2003, the United States prepared to invade Iraq. Tensions again rose against Americans living in Central Java. During that time, Paulus brought FPLAG board members to visit us in our home in Salatiga. Paulus wanted us to tell the group about MCC's longtime partnership with the Red Crescent in Iraq. Paulus, as an Indonesian Mennonite, wanted the Solo interfaith leaders to be aware that American and Canadian MCC constituents were not against Muslims and had been expressing care and concern for the people of Iraq long before the 2001 attacks on the World Trade Center and the Pentagon.

The FPLAG members asked about the possibility of contributing to needs in Iraq through MCC. We talked about MCC's website and the information about Iraq available there. Later, when afternoon prayer time came, those of our guests who were Muslim went out our front door to pray in the mosque across the street. Our all-Muslim neighborhood watched and commented. Before the group returned to Solo, our guests assured us that they would keep us informed and safe if the threat of a vocal minority against Americans worsened. The threat ebbed.

In 2004, Paulus, an Indonesian Christian, first met the militant Muslim commander, Agus. Agus's hardline Islamic radio station was broadcasting at almost the same frequency as another more moderate Muslim radio station. The conflict between the two stations turned serious. Through the interfaith forum, a moderate Muslim friend of Paulus knew of the conflict between the radio stations. He asked Paulus to help mediate. Besides his other responsibilities, Paulus is also the director of the ecumenical Christian radio station "Immanuel" in Solo. So it happened that the director of a Christian radio station stepped forward to help mediate a conflict between two Islamic radio stations.

As Paulus tells it, he was very nervous to meet with Agus for the first time. He decided to take the risk and moved to enter into the relationship. As they spent time together, the relationship strengthened between the hardline Javanese Muslim commander and the ethnic Chinese Anabaptist pastor.

In 2004, my husband Dan and I asked Paulus if we could interview him and Agus about the radio story for MCC reporting.

However, Paulus advised Dan and me that the time was not yet right for us to meet with Agus because of his hatred for Americans. As an alternative, we asked Indonesian MCC staff members Lilik Setiyanto and Abang Rahino to do the interview on the radio conflict transformation story. Paulus warned the Indonesian MCC workers not to mention that they worked with a Western Christian organization. "Just say that you are with an organization that works for peace."

As Paulus's relationship with Agus deepened, Paulus invited Agus to meet other members of FPLAG. After this exposure to Indonesian Christians and those of other faiths committed to working together, Paulus witnessed Agus becoming a different person. Paulus writes, "When you have touched a person's heart, you may be able to influence his way of thinking and way of life. [Agus's] transformation in the values of peace, plurality, and peoplehood has happened in this past year."

In spring 2005, Agus told Paulus, "If I had only known you and associated with Christians like I am doing now, I would not have needed to lose fifty of my soldiers who were killed in Ambon and Poso. I regret killing Christians."

September 2005 was again a month of tension. Small groups of militant Muslims were taking the law into their own hands to forcibly close places of worship in Solo and other parts of Java. These churches were ones the hardline groups said did not have official permission to have a place of worship.

Against the backdrop of these renewed religious tensions, Paulus invited Agus to travel with him to Aceh. Agus was asked to present a training workshop for tsunami survivors in building 1,000 simple transistor radios under the auspices of an Indonesian organization, the Forum for Humanity and Peoplehood, Indonesia (FKPI). To allow more listeners to tune into FKPI's radio show, the radios would be distributed in the barracks for displaced people. The MCC-sponsored daily call-in talk show addresses issues of trauma recovery. While teaching the radio building workshop in Aceh, Agus lived in the same house with the FKPI trauma healing facilitators and developed a close relationship with the Indonesian Christians who were a part of the team, sharing meals and many hours of late night discussions.

In September 2005, members of an MCC tour group visited the radio assembly training as Agus led the session. The visitors included both Canadians and Americans, people Agus would have refused to meet one year earlier. Agus was asked to share his impressions with the group of visiting Western Christians. As the FKPI video camera recorded, he began, "My name is Agus Hariyanto. I am happy to have this chance to go to Aceh. I am happy with my friends in FKPI and I. . . ." Agus began weeping and could not continue to talk. Then haltingly he went on speaking to the group of Americans and Canadians from MCC, "Thank you. Thank you. You are very good to come to Aceh and to help our brothers and sisters here in Aceh."

When I met up with Paulus a few days after the tour group departed, he told me more of the story. After the North American group left, the FKPI team of Muslim and Christian workers returned to the house they were sharing. Agus was asked to replay the video that had been recorded that afternoon. He watched intensely as he saw his open display of emotion on tape. Paulus whispered to him, "Why were you weeping?"

Agus replied, "I don't know. It was coming out of my heart, and I couldn't block it or stop it. I remember when I chased out the Americans. I hated them. I made war against Christians. Why are they the ones that sincerely help our brothers and sisters in Aceh? I am truly touched. I know that Americans and Christians are not like what I had thought up to now."

Paulus brought Agus and other FPLAG members to visit our MCC office in January 2006. Agus told us that because of his experiences with the interfaith forum and the work in Aceh, he is choosing to explore the path of peace with the troops he has at his command. Many of these soldiers are laborers, pedicab drivers, and parking attendants who have been recruited and trained for war. For some fighters, the experience of military training and active combat may have been the most meaningful experience of their lives. It may be difficult for them to return to more mundane "civilian" life unless better options emerge. Their commander wants them to learn about peace as a way of life.

FPLAG plans to invite the Peace Center of Duta Wacana Christian University to help conflict transformation workshops with 100 members of the militant troops at the invitation of Agus. Normally these Islamic soldiers would never have connected with a Christian resource for peacebuilding affiliated with North American Christians. But a relationship starting in the middle between moderate Indonesian Christians and moderate Indonesian Muslims has grown through networking relationships to include a militant group and a North American organization, MCC. FPLAG considers the conflict transformation workshops to be an opportunity to introduce a peacemaking alternative to violence and to model positive Muslim-Christian relationships.

THE INDONESIAN CONTEXT

Indonesia is an archipelago stretching from the Indian Ocean in the northwest to the edge of the Pacific Ocean on the east. The distance is as great as that between California and New York. The archipelago is made up of over 17,000 islands and hundreds of distinct ethnic groups. Over 220 million people are spread over the country, making Indonesia the fourth most populous nation in the world.

Over eighty percent of the people of Indonesia are followers of Islam, making Indonesia the nation with the largest population of Muslims in the world. It is important to note, however, that Indonesia is not an Islamic state. Unlike other nations of the world in which there are a majority of Muslims, Indonesia has never had an Islamic government. That said, it is also true that a complete separation of church and state or total secularism has never existed here. Islamic values, traditions, and doctrines influence daily life and politics. For those on the conservative end of the Islamic spectrum, a secular government heavily influenced by Islamic values is not enough. Some Indonesian Muslims envision an Islamic state officially governed by Islamic law.

Mennonite Central Committee is a North American organization present as a guest in a religiously charged atmosphere. MCC Indonesia connects closely with Mennonite World Conference member churches. These include the Evangelical Mennonite Church of Java (GITJ), the Muria Mennonite Church (GKMI), and the Christian Church of Indonesia (JKI). Together, these churches include about 71,300 members. The roots of the Mennonite church in Indonesia stretch back over 150 years to the first baptisms of Javanese believers, making this the oldest Mennonite church outside of Europe and North America.

Indonesian Mennonites live in an Islamic cultural context. Many of their neighbors, elected representatives, journalists, shopkeepers, teachers, and extended family members are Muslim. Interfaith relationships are a fact of life. The quality of those relationships determines the quality of their daily lives.

Most MCC workers coming for relatively short terms do not have the background to adequately understand the complexities of the religious and political situation of Indonesia. We are conscious of our position as guests who are joining in Indonesia's story for a limited period of time. As an organization, we attempt to listen and to support the priorities identified by our partners as they work for *shalom*, for peace and right relationships, through building relationships of trust among people of different faiths.

IDENTITY

It has been important for MCC Indonesia to be transparent in our identity as a Christian organization. All workers serve "in the name of Christ" as an expression of our Christian faith. As a team, we try to reflect on what God is doing in Indonesia and to take the time to be attentive to what God is doing in Indonesia. We center ourselves in Christ and the kingdom of God as the heart of our work.

MCC service workers and locally hired Indonesian Mennonite MCC staff work alongside Indonesian colleagues in partner organizations to strengthen Indonesian institutions and organizations. As MCC staff working alongside Indonesian partners of various faiths, we seek to reflect a biblical view of Christian life as the wholeness of word and deed, body and spirit, faith and life, worship and proclamation. Clearly identifying MCC's work as an expression of Christian faith is important to our witness in Indonesia.

STAKEHOLDERS

MCC Indonesia relates closely with Mennonite World Conference-affiliated synods in Indonesia. We have much in common, yet we have come to realize that North Americans and Indonesian Christians approach interfaith bridge building from different places. The history and experience of North American Anabaptists meeting Muslims is very different from the history and experience of Indonesian Mennonites who have grown up in Javanese Muslim families building relationships with Muslims. These histories in turn are also different from the history and experience of Indonesian Mennonites of Chinese descent building relationships with Javanese or Acehnese Muslims.

Most MCC workers from Canada and the United States come from home cultures in which meeting and developing relationships with Muslim people requires a concerted effort. Most of us come from a majority power position in our home countries in which a Christian-influenced culture is dominant and Islam is in a distinct minority position. We come from contexts in which many of our fellow citizens equate Islam with terrorism. In Indonesia, we serve in a context in which our Western governments, and we, as citizens, are perceived to be on a crusade against Islam. We are eager to build relationships, to dismantle the stereotypes that exist between the two cultures we have come to know. One MCC worker pointed out, "We, as bridge-builders, in some sense become the bridge."

Divisions also exist between Indonesian Muslims and Indonesian Christians, but the struggles are different. Indonesian Christians live as a minority faith among a powerful Muslim majority. Although they are Christians, much of their cultural context is heavily influenced by Islam. For many Indonesian Christians, political pluralism is viewed as a very desirable national aspiration. Pluralism provides the tolerance to allow Christians to practice their faith in peace. Other Indonesian Christians envision a time in which Indonesia moves beyond mere tolerance to a situation in which people of all faiths can work together in positive actions that build community.

Indonesian partner churches and MCC Indonesia both bring our unique, irreplaceable distinctiveness to interfaith relationships. Our agendas are different because we have different gaps to span. This has caused some tension when MCC's eagerness to build bridges of relationship directly with Muslim groups has inadvertently excluded Indonesian Christians. As we learn together, we are seeking ways to build interfaith relationships that are collaborative with Indonesian Christians rather than competitive or exclusive.

Our team is made up of educators, development workers, and administrators. We offer ourselves to work in interfaith service or to support our partners' initiatives in modeling an interfaith response to human need. Specifically, MCC works at interfaith bridge building in Indonesia in three ways:

First, MCC workers experience interfaith relationships as a part of their daily experience in Indonesia. Many MCC workers live in Muslim neighborhoods. MCC volunteers and staff work with Muslim partner organizations, Christian organizations, and interfaith organizations. Some Indonesian MCC staff members are part of Muslim extended families. Workers often have a diverse circle of friends. MCC workers seconded to universities usually have Muslim colleagues and Muslim students and participate in interfaith activities outside of school. The house helpers in MCC workers' homes may be Muslim. Two MCC workers are seconded to a Muslim organization and have moved into the household of their Muslim co-workers.

These daily relationships bring challenges and questions of identity for MCC workers whose lives are being transformed. The following comments offered by MCC workers from Canada, the United States, and Indonesia took place during MCC Indonesia team meetings in December 2005.

- One side of the question is respect for other beliefs, but the other side is fear that we could lose our distinctiveness. How do we hold the truth of Christ as the one way? If I'm not rooted, there is a fear of drifting, losing identity. It's a theological question—religious identity is at my core. How is this maintained?
- There is a point at which I am scared of losing myself— but instead of withdrawing I step forward, perhaps compromising a bit. Maybe part of the pain here is that we are transformed, that we are not who we were. If we hold on to ourselves too tightly, we miss something.
- There's also fear on the Muslim side of being Christianized. The first step to relationship is a fearful one.
- The fear is reasonable, because real engagement means there is a chance that your mind will be changed. In our house [living with Muslim colleagues] we have engaged culturally—food, language, clothing. I'm a different per-

son because of it. We haven't engaged theologically, but
I'm not sure it's a bad thing because there is a risk of conflict, of losing identity. We have to decide if the risk is
worth taking and if we are willing to be transformed.
- How is our faith formed in an interfaith context? Our
faith is hopefully in process. There's an openness to transformation in relationship. This transformation can involve becoming more like Christ or less like Christ. There
is a movement toward or away.

*A second kind of interfaith bridge building brings MCC directly in
partnership with a Muslim agency.* After the Asian tsunami of December 2004, a group of Acehnese students and academics
formed an organization to respond to the disaster. As an organization of Acehnese people, the new non-governmental organization (NGO) was, by default, shaped by the Islamic culture. The
leader of the NGO, a university professor, called an Indonesian
Mennonite leader and fellow academic to check out MCC's cre-
dentials before approaching MCC for a potential partnership in
Aceh. The leader of the new organization later told us that he
was specifically looking for an experienced international community development organization that was faith-based (as opposed to a secular organization), but which expressed its faith in
service rather than proselytizing. Through the endorsement of
an Indonesian Mennonite leader, MCC began a partnership with
this organization.

Two MCC expatriate workers live in community with their
Muslim co-workers as they implement tsunami recovery projects. One worker reflected in a report, "The members of our interfaith house listen openly to one another's religious experiences in a way often absent from intra-faith discussions. No one
asks, 'What kind of Christian are you?' It is refreshing to share
about faith in such an accepting atmosphere."

At the recommendation of Satya Wacana Christian University, MCC is supporting a member of the Liberal Islam Network
to study in the Conflict Transformation Program at Eastern Mennonite University. North American Anabaptists benefit from this
connection as he visits Christian churches and speaks to Sunday
school classes. Indonesian Christians see this support of liberal
Islam as advantageous to all Indonesian minority religions be-

cause it creates space for improved relationships between Muslims and those of other faiths in Indonesia.

The third and most important MCC Indonesia programmatic focus is supporting the interfaith networking of Indonesian partners. In these relationships, connections are built between Indonesian organizations and individuals of different faiths. For example, through Indonesian Mennonite connections, Mennonite Central Committee began a partnership with FPLAG in Solo, Central Java. This interfaith forum began when Mennonites, Catholics, Hindus, Muslims, Confucians, Buddhists, and those of traditional religions joined with the Association of Marginalized People, an NGO, to organize to distribute relief aid after the city of Solo was devastated by riots in 1999. When they completed the humanitarian response, the group decided to continue as a forum to work at ways of reducing tensions and violence in their city.

FPLAG does not attempt to come to any kind of theological consensus but instead focuses on the shared concern of peace for the city of Solo. MCC has been working with this group since 2001. The partnership has enabled the intentionally interfaith group to serve their community through supporting both ceremonial peace events in Solo and in sponsoring conflict transformation training in neighborhoods identified as experiencing high levels of tension. MCC has also sponsored emerging peace leaders recommended by FPLAG at the Summer Peacebuilding Institute at Eastern Mennonite University and the Mindanao Peacebuilding Institute in Davao, Philippines.

MCC also supports the Center for the Study and Promotion of Peace (PSPP) at Duta Wacana Christian University. The Peace Center has been heavily influenced by Indonesian Anabaptist thinking. PSPP has been invited to help conflict transformation workshops in tense areas of Indonesia. Its personnel have been invited to present workshops that include both Muslims and Christians, and they have intentionally included Muslim trainers on their roster so they can offer interfaith facilitation teams. Over the next three years, MCC will be helping the Center for the Study and Promotion of Peace launch a new interfaith peace studies graduate program.

After the tsunami, FPLAG, PSPP, and members of the theology department of Satya Wacana Christian University joined to create a forum to respond to the tsunami and earthquake in Aceh and Nias. The group set out to model an intentionally interfaith response to the trauma healing needs among survivors. The group calls itself the Forum for Humanity and Peoplehood, Indonesia (FKPI). In Aceh, a province that is almost completely Muslim, few Acehnese people personally know Christians or have ever considered the possibility that Christians and Muslims might cooperate for service. FKPI actively seeks ways to interact, connect, build trust, and share tasks of service between people of different faiths.

REFLECTIONS

All relationships carry some level of risk, uncertainty, and ambiguity. We cannot control the outcomes of our relationships. We try to listen to the ways God is leading us. In the case of the transformation of Pak Agus, what are the chances that MCC and Paulus are being duped in a big way? Did Agus really experience a transformation, or is there some hardliner strategy at work here? When we shared that story with our kids at the supper table, our son David's first response was, "That's just like the early Christians responded to Paul. When Paul first changed and stopped hunting down Christians, none of the Christians trusted him, either."

When we discussed in our MCC office whether the transformation is real, one Indonesian staff member said, "Yes, there is a possibility we might be fooled. But if we distrust, we may lose an opportunity. I choose to be optimistic." We are making a choice to believe that this is sincere. Our trust is also based on Paulus's attention to this relationship with Agus over time and his belief that the transformation is real.

Through peacebuilding work, support for leadership development, and tsunami recovery projects, MCC comes into relationship with a wide range of Muslims. Our connections include "cultural" Muslims from the academic world, Sharia law professors, members of the Liberal Islam Network, moderates, militants, and members of a sultan's family. In most cases, MCC is drawn into these relationships through the introductions and networking of our partners. We attempt to be consistently open to building relationships without "targeting" groups. As one

MCC worker noted, "That sort of objectifying—people as targets—can break the bridge. Our priority is on working together, not targeting."

We often wonder how MCC's many interfaith relationships are viewed by our Muslim friends and partners and by other Christians. What is MCC up to? What motivates us? What do we hope to accomplish by entering into these relationships? As Paulus Widjaja says, "It's not the reality but the perception that counts." One Indonesian MCC worker noted, "I have Muslim friends who think that if we want to do something [in tsunami response] we must have a goal—and that goal has been perceived to be to make Acehnese convert to Christianity."

Our real goal is faithfulness. We are called to follow Jesus, the Prince of Peace. We cannot strategize the outcomes of our relationships. But what we can control is our response to God's call in our lives and our openness to share that life in service with others. As MCC workers, we seek to bear witness to the reign of Christ in our work and relationships in Indonesia.

MCC workers do not all share the same theological viewpoint. One worker mused, "What kind of bridge are we building, since we aren't all coming from the same starting point?" As she reflected on the idea of faithfulness as our goal, another worker commented, "This takes pressure off naming a result. My goal is being a disciple."

I believe that the more points of connection with people of other faiths, the better. We know that we are called into relationship with others who are created in God's image. We know we are being mysteriously transformed as we learn from each other.

How do we know we are moving in the right direction? I imagine a visit to the optometrist in which I am sitting in front a machine testing various options for the prescription for my lenses. With each twist of the equipment, the optometrist asks, "Better? Or worse?" With the next optic adjustment, I am asked again, "Better? Or worse?" We can ask the same questions of our interfaith relationships. It this step better? Or worse?

I believe that each step toward more trusting relationships and better understanding is a move toward shalom. MCC workers are making themselves available in relationships where they work and live while remaining clear in their faith identity. Indonesian Anabaptist partners are entering into interfaith service and MCC is assisting those efforts. We know that it is good to be in situations in which we can serve together with people of other faiths.

We seek to join in faithfulness to what God is doing in Indonesia. We trust that God is at work in those interfaith relationships. We recognize that we are not in control of the results. In many cases, we don't even have enough imagination to visualize the possibilities of the work of the Holy Spirit. When I reflect on the story of Paulus and Agus, I catch a vision for how personal relationships can have an impact up to even a global level.

We offer ourselves in trusting relationships with people of other faiths, giving up control and trusting in the mystery of God to transform our diaconal service together. As Marilyn Chandler McEntyre has written,

> trust is a form of freedom. It is freedom from the need to control, and freedom from having to expend our energies proving our points and patching over the holes in our information, freedom from having to provide a fully coherent narrative, and explain away all inconvenient inconsistencies. Trust liberates us to let things be, to take our questions one at a time, to ponder them peacefully, knowing ourselves all the time to be held in the loving embrace of one who, despite not providing all the answers we want, supplies all our needs. Trust liberates us to live joyfully amid mystery. . . .[1]

As MCC workers, we try to take the time to reflect on what God is doing in Indonesia. The building trust between Pak Paulus and Pak Agus is difficult to account for. How did it happen? There is mystery and surprise. The Creator's imagination for this story is much bigger than ours.

NOTE

1. *Weavings* 21/1 (Jan.-Feb. 2006).

Chapter 2

A Fountain Flowing Deep and Wide: A Journey with Catholicism in Latin America

Susan Classen

A bridge is not built from the middle of the river.
—Ed de la Torre, Philippines

MENNONITES AND CATHOLICS: A STORY FROM NICARAGUA

After ten years in El Salvador working with the Catholic Church through Mennonite Central Committee (MCC), I wanted deeper connections with Central American Mennonites, so I began an assignment in Nicaragua. There I lived in a small village and related to the local Mennonite church. I initially lived alone but, as work developed, I requested that another MCC worker join me. The best candidate, however, happened to be Catholic. How would church members respond? When we received her application, I requested a meeting with the pastor and the leader of the women's group. I explained that the prospective new MCC worker was Catholic but wanted to live in the village and relate to the church. Both readily responded that it was no problem as long as she did not proselytize.

The new worker moved to the village and friendships quickly blossomed but, two years into her MCC term, she began to suspect that church members thought she was Mennonite. We realized that we had been mistaken when we assumed that the church leaders with whom we had spoken had explained to the congregation that she was Catholic. She then met with the pastor and expressed her desire to talk to people about her church background, since she did not want to end her three-year term knowing that her friends assumed she was Mennonite when it was not true. The pastor agreed, and a date was set for her to speak with the congregation.

As was typical in the congregation, she gave her testimony of growing up Catholic. Most of the church members had also been raised Catholic, so that came as no surprise. But when she came to the point at which people expected her to say, "and then I became Christian," she announced forthrightly, "And I'm still Catholic."

After a moment of stunned silence, one of the women spoke with conviction. "You are our 'sister'," affirming her as an accepted member of the church. Others immediately followed with their support and affirmation. "Your life shows the fruit of the Spirit so you are Christian like us," a church elder replied. "If we had been Catholic like you are Catholic, we wouldn't have needed to become evangelicals," another said. A relationship of trust and respect built over a two-year period bridged the sharp divide between Catholics and Protestants.

A phrase from a song I remember singing enthusiastically as a child has been playing in my mind as I reflect on the theme of building bridges across religious divides: "Deep and wide, deep and wide, there's a fountain flowing deep and wide." We need a deep foundation to bridge the wide span between faith traditions. Bridges are not built from the middle of a river but from the edge. We must be willing to risk living on the edge to bridge a divide. But we need a solid foundation far enough from the edge so the bridge will be strong and enduring.

DISCOVERING OUR MISSION

MCC discovers its mission as it responds to the needs around it. This missiological model of discovery provides a foundation for the current challenge of bridging faith traditions. A response to those who suffer mental illness grew out of the experience of conscientious objectors who worked in mental hospitals after World War II. Our understanding of violence has grown beyond warfare to include economic structures, institutionalized violence, and violence within families and churches, thanks in large part to the experience of MCC workers. Accompanying those who are oppressed has helped us see the connection between peacemaking and justice, moving us to advocate for those in need. We are rooted in a tradition of discovering our mission as we respond to the needs of our times.

I believe that Jesus also discovered his mission as he interacted with those around him. Matthew 15:21-28 describes an encounter with a Canaanite woman who helped Jesus break through cultural stereotypes and broaden his understanding of mission. Jesus, like all Jews of his time, was brought up with the assumption that only Jews could draw close to God. His response to a foreign woman was a socially acceptable one. He ignored her, put her down, and defined his mission in a way that excluded her. But the woman persisted until it became clear to Jesus that she was a woman of faith. The Canaanite woman was instrumental in helping Jesus realize that his mission was broader than he thought. That seed took root and grew into the early church's commitment to bridge the divide between Jews and Gentiles. We, like Jesus, discover our mission as we interact with others.

THE BROADENING OF ECUMENICAL RELATIONS

Ecumenical understanding among Mennonites has been gradually broadening for some time, and a commitment to interfaith bridge building is one more step in an ongoing process. Looking back on my life, I can see that my call to be Mennonite among Catholics is rooted in a process followed by my parents, who were changed by the ten years they spent with MCC after World War II. They, in turn, were influenced by the openness of their own parents. I find it comforting to know that I am part of something larger than my personal life choices and that the steps being made at this point in history will continue long after I am gone.

For my grandparents, ecumenism had to do with being open to Mennonites of non-Russian origin. My father, from German-speaking Russian Mennonite origin, met my mother, from English-speaking Swiss Mennonite origin, while they both served with MCC in Europe. When my father told his parents about their engagement, they responded with concern that he was involved with an "English" woman.

For my parents, ecumenism had to do with being open to Catholics. My father recounts his first experience with a Catholic priest, which made him question the closed stereotypes prevalent at the time. A group of young men uncovered a grenade while doing reconstruction work in France after World War II and were debating what to do with it when a Catholic priest walked by. The priest looked at the men and said, "You are too young to risk touching the grenade. I have lived a long, good life and I'm right with God. I will take care of it." And he did. A seed of respect for Catholics was planted in my father.

Years later my mother was asked to lead a Bible study for a group of charismatic Catholic women. The charismatic movement did a great deal to bring Catholics and Mennonites together as participants realized that the movement of the Spirit is deeper than denominational boundaries.

The Spirit leads gradually over time. My grandparents were stretched to be open to someone from a different branch of the Mennonite world. My parents were stretched to be open to Catholics. And my own experiences with MCC have taken me a step further—I am a member of a Mennonite church and an associate member of a Catholic religious community. In his letter to the Ephesians, Paul wrote that God's plan in the fullness of time is, through Christ, to gather up all things in heaven and on earth (Eph. 1:10). Ecumenical and interfaith bridge building is part of the long term "gathering" process.

REDEFINING THE DIVIDE

The division between Christian groups in North America no longer seems as wide as it once did. While the divide is sharper in Latin America, there too it is shrinking. We are discovering that denominational structures do not necessarily define with whom we feel comfortable working in partnership.

During the civil war in El Salvador (1980-1992), MCC worked in close conjunction with church partners who shared our priority of helping those in need regardless of religion or politics. MCC's commitments led to partnerships with Catholics, Lutherans, and Baptists. I was placed in a Franciscan Catholic parish because the priests and nuns were supporting rural farmers struggling to stay in their homes in the countryside as well as responding to the needs of thousands of displaced people who fled to camps in town. We were brought together by our common commitment to those in need.

I discovered that our faith-based mandate to serve "without racial, gender, religious or political qualification" had political consequences. Seventeen Catholic priests, four Catholic church women from the United States, and countless lay leaders were killed by the Salvadoran military because they were committed to the poor. A military official once declared that he knew he had found a guerrilla camp whenever soldiers discovered a picture of Monseñor Oscar Romero, the Catholic archbishop assassinated in 1980, and MCC canned meat. I remember thinking that we must be doing something right if MCC was closely associated with the archbishop I so admired for his commitment to the poor! MCC and the partners with whom we worked shared a commitment to people the government labeled "subversives." The shared theological commitment to those suffering from warfare was far deeper than doctrinal differences. We were brought together through our actions, and our partnerships were strengthened because of the risk involved.

The commitment to those suffering from the war united people and organizations across denominational boundaries. But at times that same commitment divided people *within* denominations. In 1985, I was arrested by the government military and accused of teaching Marxist doctrine. After two days, I was released by a colonel who introduced himself as a member of a Baptist church, a personal friend of Pat Robertson, and a supporter of the 700 Club. He was a member of a different Baptist church than the one with which MCC worked—in which the pastor was persecuted and one of the church members "disappeared" because of the congregation's commitment to the poor. Both the Salvadoran military official and the pastor of the congregation with which MCC worked were Baptist, but they had very different understandings of what it meant to live their faith.

Dean Brackly, a Jesuit priest living in El Salvador, summarized the question of what unites or divides people of faith. "Are victims central to the mission of the church, or are they peripheral?" That question, not doctrine or dogma, is the heart of what draws us together or pulls us apart.

DEEPER THAN DIFFERENCES

We experience unity not by denying our differences but by living our particular identity deeply and fully. Like the foundation of a bridge on the edge of a river, the roots of our own tradition ground us so that differences can be enriching rather than divisive. My faith has grown and my identity as a Christian and a Mennonite has deepened through my relationship with Catholics. Moreover, Catholic friends tell me that they have been strengthened in their faith through their relationships with Mennonites. Several novices in the Catholic religious community with whom I worked in El Salvador used to joke about being "Catholic/Mennonites." Rooted firmly in our own identities and traditions, we become open to different perspectives.

As clarity about my own particular way of living my faith has emerged, so has my respect for other ways of being faithful increased. A close Catholic friend and mentor explained ecumenism this way: "When we live our particular faith tradition to its depth, we reach the same stream of life that sustains us all." I picture it like the wells in the small Nicaraguan village where I lived. The three wells were dug at different places, but each tapped into the same vein of water winding its way underneath the surface of the village. My particular "well" is defined by my identity as a Christian, a Mennonite, and a citizen of the United States. Living that identity deeply brings me into relationship with people of other cultures, denominations, and faith traditions who also live underneath the surface. Our differences, then, become enriching reflections of diversity.

It is hard work to dig a well, though, and it is hard work to live the unity which upholds and sustains our diversity. A number of years ago I heard two men, one black and one white, speak about racism. They used the example of Paul's words to the Ephesians. "Jesus has broken down the dividing wall of hostility," they said, "but there is still a great deal of rubble to shovel."

I remember arriving in San Salvador the day after a major earthquake demolished significant areas of the city. I felt overwhelmed by the massive amounts of debris blocking the streets. The bus took one street after another trying to find one that was open. Finally I had to get off and walk. I can still see the dazed residents slowly picking through the mounds of rubble. That is the mental image that comes to mind when I think of the walls of hostility being torn down.

Where do we start when the "debris" that divides us is overwhelming? I guess we start, like the earthquake victims, by slowly clearing the area directly surrounding us. The following are examples of the slow, painstaking work of clearing the rubble so that unity can grow.

Many ways of praying

I learned through experience that my way of praying is not the only way. I was seconded to a Catholic parish health program in El Salvador and, due to the conflict, the only way I could visit outlying towns and villages was with the priest when he went to say mass. I was in the small town of Cacaopera one Sunday morning when we heard shooting during the service. As the shots came closer, several men quietly got up and closed the heavy, wooden church doors. Soon the shots were so close that I wondered if the bullets were hitting the doors. The people around me remained calm. No one gave instructions, but they all seemed to know what to do. They simply lay down on the floor and began reciting the rosary. The rise and fall of the repetitive prayer calmed my racing heart. I experienced the power of a way of praying that I had previously assumed was not meaningful.

Deeper than doctrine

I was respectful of Catholic teaching that only Catholics participate in communion and, for the first year, I had no desire to do so. But over a period of time I realized that, despite our theological differences, I felt as if we were in fellowship with each other, and I wanted to express it in some way. One evening, those of us who worked in the parish gathered for a special mass for the brother of one of the nuns who had just been killed by the military. The group was small, about fifteen of us. I longed to participate in the breaking of the bread but felt that I needed to respect their position regarding non-Catholics. After the service, one of the more traditional sisters approached me and said that, despite what canon law dictates, it was not right for me to be left out. Bridge building goes both ways. We were all becoming more open as we came to trust each other.

The Central American Anabaptist Peace Network

The REDPAZ is a Central American Anabaptist peace network which began with MCC support. It brings together participants from Central America and Mexico for a series of ten, one-week conflict transformation workshops spread over two years. As I looked around the circle during one course, I thought that this must be what Paul meant when he said that in the body of Christ there is no longer Jew or Greek, slave or free, male or female (Gal. 3:28). I saw indigenous persons and Latinos, women and men, Catholics and "evangelicals" (the term used for all Protestants). I saw representatives from each of the Central American countries and Mexico. I saw people from all walks of life united by their commitment to work for peace.

The spirituality for peacemakers workshops came toward the end of the two-year training period. As I spoke with other facilitators, I realized that the group cohesion I experienced was the fruit of the previous workshops. Over time, participants experience a reality deeper than the cultural, political, and theological differences which divide them and the societies they represent. Trust and respect is built and the groups become a microcosm of the change they seek to bring about as they work toward building a culture of peace.

I remember watching a Mennonite pastor whom I had known before he participated in the REDPAZ courses. Before the training, he held a traditional evangelical view that Catholics needed to convert to Christianity. I was struck, then, to observe that he had become close friends with a leader of a Catholic Christian Base Community. So much trust had grown between them that they were comfortable joking about their differences. At the end of the training, the pastor explained that his view of

social issues. My base community neighbors in El Salvador have a broad understanding of social issues, but the personal lives of many are in shambles. We need both.

I used to think that the personal and social aspect of our faith should be balanced within each congregation and denomination. Now I am not so sure. Maybe the balance comes in the big picture. Perhaps the gift of the evangelical church to the global body of Christ has to do with the transforming power of the Spirit in our individual lives which is held in tension by the gift of the base community perspective of God's concern for social justice. If that is the case, then we need a great deal of humility in our relationships with each other as we recognize that God leads in diverse ways.

My own experience with the Catholic church grew out of MCC's principles, and my heartfelt search for God inspired by my life and work first in Bolivia and then in El Salvador. My commitment to a Mennonite understanding of service gave me the energy to push through the mourning after my mother's death at the beginning of my first term in Bolivia, through six years of war in El Salvador, and through the grief after my father's death. The energy I could muster from trying to do what I believed was right, however, eventually gave out. Then I searched for the God who authentically responds to people amid suffering.

I realized I needed help to cope with the intensity of what I was experiencing but I did not know what to do or where to go. When a Catholic sister who was a friend and co-worker suggested I go to her motherhouse, I readily accepted. Her community, the Sisters of Loretto, took me in for an extended time of rest and renewal. During that difficult time the Catholic spiritual tradition put me in touch with God's unconditional love and became instrumental in sustaining my commitment to service. I am a better Mennonite because of my relationship with Catholics.

Bridges are built on deep foundations. MCC programs are not shallow projects or ends in and of themselves. At their best, they are expressions of incarnate love and manifestations of the dreams that God plants within us for a world that is just. Any of our programs build bridges when they are authentic expressions of love.

"Deep and wide. Deep and wide. There's a fountain flowing deep and wide. . . . " May we drink from the fountain that flows from an Infinite Source which, at its depth, unites us all.

Chapter 3

Christian-Muslim Relations in Nigeria: Mennonite Central Committee and Multi-Faith Peacebuilding

Gopar Tapkida

WHERE DO WE BEGIN?
RESPONDING TO THE JOS CRIS

My family and I had arrived in Jos in Plateau State, Nigeria, in August 2001, just one month before multi-ethnic riots gripped the region from September 7 to 12, 2001. I had been away from Nigeria for graduate studies in peace and conflict transformation at Eastern Mennonite University in Virginia. We were still living in a guesthouse when intense fighting began between the Hausa Muslims and the Christian communities. Many lost their lives in the clash. Millions of dollars worth of homes, churches, mosques, and vehicles were burned.

The whole of Jos was filled with smoke rising from every direction. For six days movement was restricted and highly risky.

On the second day of the crisis, unknown persons shot down two guards of the guesthouse where my family and I were taking refuge. The various hospitals in Jos city were filled with people who had been badly wounded in the violence. Many took refuge at various police and military barracks. With the help of security agents, some mission groups withdrew from Jos to Abuja (the Nigerian capital, a city about 300 kilometers south west of Jos). The situation compelled us into compulsory fasting, since we could not buy foodstuffs. We were also terrified, especially with the sound of gunshots all day and all night.

When the dust of the violence started settling down, my wife Monica and I went out to see the ruins. We could not stop weeping. We became stunned and quickly withdrew to the guesthouse. We soon realized that Monica had lost three cousins. The friend who had printed our wedding cards had been killed, butchered beyond recognition. These were only a few among many people we knew who lost their lives in the crisis. Passion for vengeance ran high among victims from both sides of the divide. The wounds were deep, and the pains were unbearable.

The ugliness of the Jos crisis lies not only in the number of lives lost and the level of destruction to goods and property, but even more in the dreadful ways in which people were killed, cut into pieces, and burnt and roasted almost like barbeque. Survivors could not imagine associating their loved ones with such images. This lengthened the period of pain and trauma as people's imaginations were filled with all kinds of denials and fantasies. As a trained peace practitioner, I soon began to realize I was alone. I saw myself as someone swimming in an ocean alone and not knowing which direction I was going, with nothing for me to hold onto for survival. Everything was so complex and impossible. *"Where do we begin?"* was the question.

MENNONITE CENTRAL COMMITTEE IN NIGERIA

For me, "where to begin" has meant working to shape the multi-ethnic peacebuilding program of Mennonite Central Committee (MCC). MCC has worked in Nigeria for over four decades, developing a wide network of friendships and partnerships with Nigerian churches, church-related groups, and civil society institutions. The depth and breadth of MCC's presence in the country have put MCC in a position to respond to interfaith tensions that have gripped Nigeria over the past years.

In 1963, MCC was invited by the Nigerian government to place teachers in northern Nigeria through MCC's Teachers Abroad Program (TAP). The government hoped to close the educational gap between northern and southern Nigeria through this initiative. The TAP initiative led to MCC's longer-term involvement and also cemented MCC's foundational mode of operation in Africa—secondment of personnel and funding of African initiatives, supporting and serving through the existing structures of Nigerian churches and Nigerian organizations.

Since 1963 MCC Nigeria has remained committed to working alongside partners at their invitation. Present program efforts of MCC in Nigeria include theological education, support for agricultural development, technical assistance, income generation, peace education, health and handicapped services. MCC responds to the invitations of Nigerian institutions in program areas that intersect with MCC's global priorities of relief, community development, and peacebuilding. MCC chooses to stand in solidarity with Nigerians working at structural injustice and seeks to build personal relationships shaped by a willingness to learn from every culture, community, and person as a source of wisdom.

THE JOS CONFLICT:
SYMPTOM OF A WIDER PROBLEM

Jos was not the only town in Nigeria to experience the kind of violence that scarred the area in September 2001. Since the 1999 elections, more than 10,000 persons have been killed in various communal crises. Although some Nigerian states have witnessed more of these crises than Plateau State, the crisis in Plateau State posed a threat to national security due to its cosmopolitan nature. Jos is one of the most diverse cities in Nigeria, thanks to mass migration into the area during the tin mining boom at the turn of the nineteenth century. Plateau State had also attracted a large population of Nigerians and other nationals due to its peacefulness and pleasant climate.

But on May 18, 2004, the Nigerian President, Chief Olusegun Obasanjo, declared a state of emergency in Plateau State because of what he termed "mutual genocide" precipitated by the ethno-religious disturbances in the town of Yelwa. He stressed that the governor and the political leaders in Plateau were incapable of handling the crisis. By this declaration, the governor, his deputy, and the state house of assembly were suspended for six months, and retired Major General Mohammed C. Alli was made the Sole Administrator of Plateau State. Obasanjo justified the declaration on the grounds that it would serve as a deterrent to all state governors in Nigeria.

The crisis in Plateau State is typical of current realities in many parts of Nigeria—latent tensions waiting for a spark to ignite violence. Fundamental to peacebuilding is conceptualizing peace not only as the absence of violence but also as the presence of justice. True peace encompasses not only the restoring of calm but also addresses the trauma needs of victims and injustice in the aftermath of conflict or as the antecedent of conflict.

If we want to understand the current inter-ethnic and inter-religious crises in Nigeria, and if we as peacebuilders wish to be successful in transforming these conflicts, we must first know our history. The current crises are the products, as I noted briefly above, of latent tensions. Where, we must ask, do these tensions come from? After sketching a brief history of religion and colonialism in Nigeria, I will outline what I believe is a transformational approach to peacebuilding in a context of interfaith tension and violence.

RELIGION, COLONIALISM, AND INDEPENDENCE: THE NIGERIAN CASE

Islam arrived in northern Nigeria between the fourteenth and fifteenth centuries through the movement of merchants, judges, scholars, and missionaries. It spread gradually in the north of Nigeria through trans-Saharan trade. It grew mainly among the Hausa/Fulani tribes until the Islamic jihad (struggle) led by Usman Dan Fodio against the non-Muslim communities in north and the Middle Belt of Nigeria in the eighteenth century. This jihad brought the fragmented non-Muslim groups in the north and some parts of the Middle Belt of Nigeria under the control of a powerful Islamic bloc. Along with Islam, the Hausa language and culture and the political structure of the caliphate came to dominate much of Nigeria, marginalizing numerous smaller ethnic groups.[1]

The eighteenth-century jihad introduced several innovations into northern Nigeria: central Islamic authority; an administrative apparatus; and judicial institutions that cut across ethnic boundaries and set aside and opposed existing non-Muslim institutions. When colonial administrators arrived in northern Nigeria between 1900 and 1903, they were vehemently resisted by the Islamic leadership and had to adopt what later came to be known as "indirect rule." This was a philosophy of governing colonies as much as possible through the native people. Most ethnic groups in the north, however, had already been colonized by the Hausa/Fulani. Therefore, the native authorities appointed by the British colonial administrators did not truly represent the indigenous people they were administering.

The theory of indirect rule in the non-Muslim areas required that British bayonets maintain the Muslim Fulanis in power over an unwilling and unconquered people. The placement of non-Muslim areas under Fulani emirate rule was usually justified on the grounds that it was difficult to identify efficient indigenous chiefs. Hence, the emirs became "British junior partners" in governing other peoples.[2] This leadership disparity continues to be a major root cause of violent conflict in the north and the Middle Belt of Nigeria.

Although Christian mission societies began work among Nigeria's coastal communities between 1841 and 1875, it wasn't until the beginning of the twentieth century that the Christian missionaries reached the interior communities. When the Christian missionaries first came to Nigeria in the nineteenth century, they initially spread only in the areas under direct control of the colonial administrators. Christianity did not find roots in the north because of treaties between the British colonialists and the Islamic leaders which preserved Islamic rule and prohibited other religions. Since Christianity also came with Western education and medical facilities, its rejection in the north deprived the region of these vital infrastructures.

The legacies of Islamic invasion, the colonial leadership disparity, and the activities of the early Christian missionaries have all contributed to current conflicts in multiple ways. First, the minority communities are asking questions about the fairness of the native authority systems because they seem to have provided undue advantages to a select group of people. As attempts are made to challenge these systems, many Nigerians are surprised to discover that the controverted issues have already been settled in the country's constitution. Second, the leadership disparity created by this historical legacy and the subsequent scramble for power among the so-called nationalists immediately after independence further resulted in coups, counter-coups, and the Nigerian civil war in the 1960s. Since the civil war (1967-1970), the military has remained in power and ruled Nigeria almost continuously until 1999, when Nigeria elected a civilian government.

During this period, the military consciously or unconsciously militarized not just the government but also Nigerian civil society. Therefore, although now Nigeria is under a democratic government, only the political uniform has changed. The political and administrative office holders and Nigerian policies have not. Finally, when the British carved the physical entity of Nigeria out of the colonially administered lands, they paid no particular attention to the needs and physical location of the various ethnic groups already residing there. Not surprisingly, the current Nigerian democratic dispensation has forced a surprising recognition of the daunting task entailed in nation-building in the face of the tremendous diversity of ethnic groups, languages, visions of nationhood, and severe religious and political tensions.

TRANSFORMATIONAL PEACEBUILDING AMID NIGERIA'S MULTI-FAITH REALITY

The Islamic consolidation of power in northern Nigeria, the legacy of British colonialism, and the history of Christian missions all, therefore, factor into the current conflicts plaguing Nigeria, in which definitions of the nation and the shaping of government institutions are hotly contested. As the massacres in Jos in 2001 sadly attest, these conflicts can turn and have turned deadly. How, peacebuilders must ask, can the current conflicts be transformed? How can we work toward a positive vision of Nigeria in which persons from differing religions and ethnic backgrounds might live together in peace?

Governmental and some non-governmental agencies have adopted a number of approaches to address the conflict in Jos and other parts of Nigeria. Most of these approaches, I argue, were non-transformational. MCC, on the other hand, has sought to adopt a transformational approach. In the remainder of this chapter, I describe transformational approaches to peacemaking and contrast them with non-transformational approaches.

Important to multi-faith peacebuilding is the transformation of institutions as well as individuals within the institutions. Institutional transformation however, does not only refer to institutions changing their programs and adopting peacebuilding activities. Even more, it refers to the transformation of institutional vision and values for the common good of people beyond the institutions.

In its multi-faith peacebuilding endeavors in Nigeria, MCC hopes to create an atmosphere where everyone encounters and discovers one another in the dialogue session. It enables participants to carry with them the potential for personal transformation. MCC works inter-ethnically, interreligiously, and among a variety of cultures with a lowkey approach. Publicity is avoided where possible, with a preferred focus on grassroots participation. This approach stands in contrast to high-powered government intervention, often carried out by people unaffected by the trauma of violent encounter.

A transformational approach to peacemaking is strategic. The direction of the workshops is determined by the participants. Peace trainings are done in phases, allowing participants to process the learning over time, returning to their villages, towns, and cities with curiosity and a new set of lenses to see dynamics within their families, their neighborhoods, and larger landscapes. Participants decide on strategies through learning from one another, building trust, and recognizing misconceptions and stereotypes which hinder peaceful coexistence.

MCC multi-faith peacebuilding is designed to provide both personal and systemic transformation. This transformation usually begins when participants come to realize that victims on the other side of the divide are also suffering. With well-guided strategies, participants come to see themselves as both the source of the conflict as well as the potential resource for building sustainable peace. The potential for renewal, for hope, and for transformed vision and insight is often remarkable. The story of Amina Ahmad is one among many shining examples of the impact of MCC multi-faith peacebuilding in Nigeria.

Amina Ahmad graduated from university with a bachelor's degree in education several years ago. She was born and raised in Jos. During the conflict there in 2001, her uncle was killed and his house totally destroyed. Her oldest brother was killed, her family shopping complex was burnt to ashes, and their family home in Wase was destroyed. Amina became infuriated with Christians and decided to do everything possible to destroy Christianity in Plateau State and Nigeria as a whole. She joined a violent group in Jos, was offered a paid job with them, and was also trained in the use of guns, fetish-charms, and other means of self-protection from and fighting against Christians.

Amina was invited to an MCC-assisted multi-faith peacebuilding workshop in October 2003. Amina later said that she initially resisted coming to the workshop because she had taken an oath to have nothing to do with Christians and the workshop was organized by a Christian agency (the Jos Catholic Diocese Justice Development and Peace Commission) and held in a Christian-dominated area. For some reason, her father convinced her to attend the workshop. She did so, but with great cynicism. According to Amina, she arrived at the workshop venue with all her charms ready for action: if she didn't approve of the workshop, she would be able to use these fetish-charms to curse the facilitators and other participants. To worsen matters, the facilitators—Yakubu Joseph and Gopar Tapkida—were both Christians working for a Christian organization, MCC. Amina adopted wait-and-see tactics before taking action.

Early in the workshop, participants shared their hopes and fears. Amina expressed her hostility toward Christians and stressed that she hoped that no one would attempt to convert her to Christianity. The first day passed with Amina saying nothing more. The second day also came and went without further input.

On the third day, Amina stood up to speak. Everyone was nervous, expecting her to rock the boat of the entire multi-faith peacebuilding process. Contrary to this expectation, Amina said, "I wish to make it abundantly clear that I have forgiven those Christians who killed my uncle and my brother and burnt our houses and our shop. I do not blame them for such nasty behavior. I see their action as a result of societal ills, and I am part of that construction. I will go home and work for peace." We could sense Amina's pain as she spoke and see the tears running down her face. Amina was not the only person who experienced personal transformation at this workshop. We all did, but her confession came to us facilitators as a great surprise, given some of the things she had shared in her earlier introduction. As facilitators, we suspected that her confession was coming from emotion rather than from true conviction.

Amina returned home at the end of the workshop and immediately started peacebuilding work among her colleagues. She was accused of having been bribed with huge amounts of money by the Christians and was threatened with the loss of her job if she would not stop the "so-called" peace work. Amina persisted and consequently lost her job. She came to the MCC office with her termination letter and said, "Although the challenges of multi-faith peace work are great, having been transformed from within, it is much easier for me to pursue peace work than to pretend and do otherwise. This is because doing otherwise will mean denying my transformed identity which is harder by far." Today, Amina, in conjunction with other Muslim women, has established the Association of Concerned Community Women (ACCW) with the sole aim of training Muslim women and Muslim communities on issues around multi-faith peacebuilding and HIV/AIDS awareness and prevention.

Multi-faith peace work is highly sensitive. Building trust requires long periods of time. Participants have to trust the process to even begin the journey toward the envisioned desired future. Peacebuilders need to engage people with dedication, care, openness, and attentiveness. We have to use a language that communicates to the hearts of our hearers.

A number of things can help us do this. First, we ourselves have to be transformed. We cannot give what we do not have. Second, multi-faith peacebuilding is not to be based on theory or technique. Instead, it must be based on personal conviction and commitment. Theories are not what bring about the zealous behaviors and commitment often associated with religion. Suicide bombings spring from sincere conviction. Finally, the gift of relationship in multi-faith peacebuilding does not end along with a successful workshop. Connections remain and continue to grow.

Above all, those who experience transformation during the training are exposed to various challenges that often accompany every start of a new journey. Authentic peacebuilding includes persistent long-term support. It is not about changing the whole world in one day. This is unlike governmental agencies, whose lifespan lasts only as long as the state constitution stipulates. In such cases, the regime often limits its concern to things that could contribute to immediate results, since that is what adds to the regime's credibility and legitimacy. Activities that bring results beyond the lifespan of a given governmental administration are less attractive to the powers that be, because such things might be credited to the next regime at the expense of their own.

The transformational paradigm further stresses a critical strategic adaptability of multi-faith peacebuilding endeavors. MCC effectively applies adaptable approaches when workshops are held in a local setting with facilitators willing to stay in village housing instead of upscale hotels. This willingness validates "our neighbor." Contextualized local materials and the flexibility so necessary to the work of connecting with people are used in presentations. This means meeting under a tree at one time and another time using PowerPoint presentations at a hotel in Abuja (the capital of Nigeria). Each training session has its own training materials designed specifically for the target audience. This recognizes the sensitivity of religious conflict and avoids the risk of generalization. This also enables facilitators to elicit stories from participants and encourage the hearing of one another's experiences so as to learn from and remind each other of strengths and frailties, similarities and differences, hopes and dreams, expectations and disappointments.

MCC operating principles also state a commitment to collaboration. That is, we try to give people who would not normally interact with one another the opportunity to meet, share ideas, and learn to accept and creatively deal with differences. Forums on peacebuilding that segregate based on societal roles and positions, religious affiliation, or gender reduce opportunities for effective integration. Government agencies like ECOWAS (Economic Community of West African States) and the African Union have a highly political top-down approach to peacebuilding which has led to relative calm in some countries but often without the sort of transformation within communities that can ensure its sustainability.

When grassroots members, ethnic/religious leaders, academics, humanitarian leaders, political and military leaders all convene together to listen to one another and brainstorm solutions to ongoing tensions, the real reasons for conflict are brought to the fore. The gross assumption that the political class represents their grassroots constituencies becomes a reason for excluding the grassroots from participating in organized state peace processes. However, our experience has shown that when people are victimized in crises, their identities change significantly, and what matters most is their new identities as victims or survivors. Hence, those who could truly represent them would be fellow survivors of similar crisis.

Another myth is the assumption that grassroots people are not educated and so would not be articulate when it comes to negotiation. Again, experience has shown that the problem is not with the level of education of the grassroots. Instead, the problem lies with the way these tables of negotiation are designed. The tables are designed for a contest of wills instead of for transformation.

Individuals involved in the conflict are disenfranchised when peacebuilding processes regard them as "troublemakers" (because of the accumulated energy for vengeance) and "beggars" (because they have lost everything), instead of including them as resources for peacebuilding. It is the accumulated energy, intensified by victimhood, which sustains the circle of violence at the crisis stage of conflict. One of MCC's main approaches to peace work is adopting a transformational approach in which survivors of crises are regarded as major resources for constructing a vision for peace. It is necessary to see people not as beggars or troublemakers but as stakeholders and people of potential transformation.

Speaking to the major motivation behind MCC involvement in multi-faith peacebuilding in Nigeria, Joanna Bergen stresses that

> Underlying all program values of MCC is commitment to God through faith. Micah 6:8 states "He has told you, O mortal what is good; and what does the Lord require of you but to do justice, and to love kindness and to walk humbly

with your God?" A belief in the God of justice, kindness, and humility is affirmed through the person of Jesus Christ. Jesus informs our actions—the Jesus of the Christian Scriptures espouses the love of neighbor, even enemy (Matt. 5: 43-44). Through Jesus the storyteller, we read the call to give food to the hungry, drink for the thirsty, clothes for the naked and care for the imprisoned (Matt. 25:31-45).

ISSUES AND CHALLENGES IN MCC'S INTERFAITH WORK IN NIGERIA

Numerous challenges await the multi-faith peace facilitator. Jesus said, "The prophet is without honor in his own home." This was a common experience when we started the work of multi-faith peacebuilding in Nigeria. It did not take us long to realize that those who are transformed—those who build bridges across religious and ethnic divides—are also often referred to by their colleagues as "betrayers, hypocrites, and people with watered-down faith." Other challenges include mistaking peace for passivity or cowardice; a tendency to explain the current crisis as a sign of the end times, thereby encouraging people to wait for some kind of divine intervention rather than actively being involved in multi-faith peacebuilding; and advocating for "self-defense" theology which undermines Jesus' basic sermons on nonviolent peacebuilding.

The globalization of religious sentiments, such as the so-called war on terror, and the contagious nature of ethno-religious conflict, combined with the language of self-preservation at all costs, infects entire ethno-religious communities. This fogs the economic and political issues that underlie crises. Hardline stances further discourage multi-faith initiatives and disallow friendship and fellowship, making it hard at times for persons of differing religious backgrounds to eat and be in one place together.

Poverty also fosters fundamentalism and intolerance within the Christian and Muslim communities. Issues such as land disputes, access to resources, rapid urbanization, and drastic economic fluctuations need to be addressed through civil education, poverty mitigation programs, relief, advocacy, research, and documentation. The scope of the pressing tasks can be daunting, and religious organizations like MCC have limited financial means to address them.

The Islamic invasion of Nigeria, the colonial leadership disparity, and the coming of the early Christian missionaries created legacies that have served as a fertile breeding ground for ethno-religious conflict in Nigeria. This can be seen in the political advantages accorded one section of the country above others and the educational advantages of another section over others. All these have led to educational, economic, political, and social gaps between the Christian South/non-Muslim groups, on the one hand, and the Muslims in the north on the other.

MCC's years of experience in multi-faith peacebuilding in Nigeria have taught us that the point of entry for any effective multi-faith peace effort is, above all, a commitment to the people, more than an undue focus on objectives and activities. Both victim and perpetrator are key factors in successful personal and community transformation. However, reconstructing a community for the common good of people should not be left in the hands of only a few individuals. Everybody has something to contribute, and this can be achieved through integrated approaches that involve entire communities. As many of the players in a given conflict as possible should participate, both highly visible people with power and people at the grassroots: average men and women, community leaders, traditional and religious leaders.

It is also vital to focus on strategic and qualitative approaches with a long-term vision while also implementing short-term activities that gradually lead to the desired future. Short-term setbacks should be viewed not as the final indicators of failure but as opportunities for reviewing our programs and assumptions, opportunities to listen more carefully to communities in conflict to determine how best to proceed. Multi-faith peace work has both short-term and long-term dimensions— perhaps with fewer successes within one's own life than one might hope!

Religious organizations do well to see multi-faith peacebuilding as important in its own right. Intentional proselytizing alienates key players in the peace process. Although the art of proselytizing usually comes from a loving heart, it is often the most misunderstood activity and often leads to a painful ending.

Multi-faith peacebuilding, I believe, is a valid end in itself, a means to connect people across religious divides, to build relationships and foster hope—thus answering the call of Jesus to feed, clothe, and visit "our neighbor," regardless of whether the neighbor is Christian or Muslim.

NOTES

1. Y. Turaki, *The Colonial Legacy in Northern Nigeria* (Jos, Nigeria: Challenge Press, 1993), 42.

2. Turaki, 67-68.

Chapter 4

Reflections on Mennonite Interfaith Work in Somalia

Chantal Logan

*F*or over five decades, Mennonite Christians and Somali Muslims have developed strong bonds of friendship and trust, thanks to the work of Eastern Mennonite Missions and Mennonite Central Committee. These relational bonds have been strengthened not only by tragic events, such as the murder of mission worker Merlin Grove, but also by risk-taking mission policies, such as allowing Islam to be taught in mission schools. In this chapter, I describe the history of these Christian-Muslim relationships forged by Mennonite mission and aid workers and make a plea for maintaining this interfaith bridge.

ISLAM AND SOMALIS

If one looks at any book about Somali identity, especially books written before 1995, three phrases consistently recur: "one language, one culture, one religion." The Somali people are always presented as being a homogeneous group. Now, after fifteen years of civil war and the absence of a central government, some Somali scholars are questioning the idea of homogeneity.

But for years the Somalis have presented and perceived themselves as a homogeneous group. They have insisted that one element of their homogeneity is their religion. All Somalis are Muslims, they emphatically declare. In other words, being Somali is synonymous with being Muslim. How, then, did the Somalis become Muslim?

If one asks Somalis, they usually give the traditional view. According to their genealogies, their ancestor came from Saudi Arabia. This ancestor, sometimes portrayed as a Muslim missionary, brought Islam to the people in Somalia. Once there, he married a local woman, and from that marriage came the Somali people.

Anthropologists often tell a different story. They explain that the Somalis probably came from the high plateau of Ethiopia and migrated down into the Horn of Africa. There is even evidence, according to one Somali historian, that in the fifteenth century some members of Somali clans were of Christian ancestry and therefore would not join Muslim chief "Mohamed the Left-Handed" in his fight against Ethiopian Christians.[1] What he says may be true, but the story that people tell about themselves and who they perceive to be is much more important than what scholars tell us, especially if one is to understand contemporary issues.

CHRISTIANITY AND SOMALIS

When the European colonial powers came to the Horn of Africa in the nineteenth century, they did not find a Christian church as they had in the Middle East or in Ethiopia (Abyssinia then), where the history of the Christian church reaches back centuries. In Somalia, the Christian presence came with European colonization and arrived via two main groups. The first were the Italian Catholics who came on the heels of colonization. Second were the Mennonites and a few other Protestant groups who arrived only a few years before Somalia's independence.

The Somali territory, like most other parts of Africa, was carved out by the colonial powers—in this case the British, the Italian, and the French. The British controlled the northern region and, as in northern Nigeria and other parts of their empire where Muslims were a majority, the British prohibited Christian missions to operate. They did so because they feared the reaction of the local people.

But there were no such restrictions in the southern, Italian-controlled part of Somalia. The Catholic church was allowed to work freely. Although Italy was defeated in the Second World War, the Italians were allowed to maintain jurisdiction over southern Somalia under a United Nation trusteeship. When the Mennonites came to Somalia in 1954, they went to the Italian trusteeship, because the British would not have allowed them to establish themselves in the north.

The Mennonites—representing Eastern Mennonite Board of Missions and Charities, the mission agency of the Lancaster Conference—built schools and hospitals and engaged in mission work. By the time Somalia became independent in 1960, with the new Somali regime gradually restricting freedom of religion, the Mennonite mission was already well established.

BUILDING TRUST
BETWEEN MENNONITES AND SOMALIS

The first post-independence stipulation by the new Somali government was that Islam be the only religion of the country. Later the government added a clause to the declaration stating that it was illegal to proselytize (for Christians, but not for Muslims) in Somalia. The change did not greatly affect the Mennonite mission. The schools had become well-known among and accepted by Somalis, and Mennonite workers had always been relatively circumspect in their witnessing.

The mission, however, came to a decisive crossroad when the government issued another regulation declaring that Islam had to be taught in all schools. The Mennonite Somali story could have come to an end at that point if the Mennonites had decided, like other Protestant missions, to close their schools. But even though this was a Christian mission, the Mennonite missionaries in Somalia, after consultation with new Somali believers and with the approval of the Lancaster Conference mission board, decided that the schools would remain opened and Islam would be allowed to be taught.

This decision represented a ground-breaking moment in the relationship between Somalis and Mennonites. The Somalis recognized that Mennonites had come to serve and not just to convert them. If they had come just to convert, they would have left or closed their schools. Even today, Somalis still cite this moment as establishing among Somalis deep trust in Mennonite work.

Another event, this one tragic, also helped build trust. One of the Mennonite missionaries, Merlin Grove, was killed by an Islamic fundamentalist. Some people expected that the Mennonites would leave because of the danger. The Mennonite missionaries, however, did not leave. The decision to stay communicated a dual message of commitment to the Somali people and of forgiveness of enemies. Although those two events happened more than thirty years ago, Somalis still remember and retell them today. They are part of the reason Mennonites and Somalis have the kind of relationship they do, one that allows Mennonites to work freely among the Somalis.

But of course there were other milestones. Most importantly, in 1975 all Mennonites were expelled from Somalia, more for political than religious reasons. At that time Somalia had close ties with the Soviet Union, and since Mennonites were North Americans, they were suspected of being CIA agents.

In 1980, however, the Mennonite mission was asked to return when government policy shifted and Somalia aligned itself with the United States. Since all the schools started by Eastern Mennonite Board of Missions and Charities (now Eastern Mennonite Missions, or EMM) had been nationalized, the Eastern board personnel came back but worked in governmental schools under the Somali Ministry of Education. (They also did medical work as they had done when they first came.) Around this time MCC became active in refugee work because the war with Ethiopia in 1977 had brought a flood of refugees into Somalia. In 1990, when the government collapsed, MCC and EMM (EMBMC at the time) initiated a joint Somalia program.

Because the Mennonites have such a good reputation, when we travel to Somalia today, , many things done by other Christian missions are attributed to Mennonites. The people would tell us, "You had a school in such and such a place" and we would say, "No, no, that was not us." In Somalia, the name *Mennonite* has become synonymous with Christian mission. The Mennonites superseded others not because they were better people but because of their theology. They were able to develop a theology not only of presence and commitment but also of sacrifice and forgiveness. This made it easier for them to make the right choices.

MCC AND EMM WORK SINCE THE CIVIL WAR

In 1990, when the civil war started in Somalia, nobody thought anarchy would last until today. Nobody was prepared for the fact that there wouldn't be a central government for so many years. The length of the war took United Nations agencies, international non-governmental organizations (NGOs), and church-related groups like the Mennonites by surprise. They scrambled to know how to intervene. Knowing how to respond was difficult because of the absence of an official government.

The Mennonites, with their long history in Somalia, had an advantage here. Their knowledge of the people and their culture helped them work through unofficial channels, but above all they were seen by the Somalis not as an external agency but as a group of people who had already gained the trust of the people. In the absence of official government structures, trust became everything.

When the international community intervenes in disaster areas, especially in the absence of government, it works primarily through NGOs. To receive help or funding for their projects, local people have to create an NGO, adopt an NGO structure, or learn how to relate to the big international NGOs. It is ironic that the ones who need the help have to adapt to the ones who provide it rather than the other way around. Because Mennonites had established relationships with the Somalis, they could use other channels. Especially in peacebuilding, the area in which MCC and EMM focused their work, it was possible to support peace conferences, particularly at the local level, by working through councils of elders native to the region rather than newly created artificial NGOs which wanted to do peace work. The longevity of Mennonite presence in the country, coupled with the trust Mennonites had gained from Somalis over the years, gave Mennonites knowledge of Somali structures other international groups lacked.

For some international NGOs, which considered themselves neutral because they were secular, it was hard to understand that a religious organization like MCC could be regarded as a valuable and trusted partner by Somalis. They had difficulty seeing that it was because we were a religious people that the Somalis appreciated working with us. The international NGOs envied our relations of partnership with Somalis but did not understand how these relationships had been forged.

When I was teaching in Djibouti, an Islamic country, I learned that Muslims appreciated knowing my faith commitment. I was teaching in the local schools with other French government teachers, many of whom were atheists or agnostics. I was working under EMM, a Christian agency, and I spoke a religious language. Muslim colleagues, students, and neighbors thus looked to me as somebody with whom they had something in common. Like them, I believed in God, and we could connect because we shared a religious world view. Like other Mennonite workers in Somalia, I found out working with Somali partners that overt use of religious language was an advantage in building trust and relationships.

This was not "interfaith dialogue," but it was interfaith bridge building, because we were an acknowledged Christian group relating to an Islamic people. "Acknowledged" is crucial, because the one thing worse than an infidel for a Muslim is a hypocrite. Those who disguise their Christian identity (either at the personal or agency levels) are much more despised than those who acknowledge it openly.

The interfaith dimension of our work was more obvious when we sent Somalis to Christian peace workshops in Zambia. Because transparency and integrity are important, we made it clear to the Somali trainees that they were going to a Christian peacebuilding institute. We warned them that there would be a chapel and a Christian framework. We were also concerned about how they would be received by the people at the institute who were all Christian. The first person we sent was so enthusiastic about what he had learned that he called home while the program was still in session and reported what those back home should be doing to resolve one of their struggles.

We were also pleased to see that the Zambians who were in charge of the institute gave him a chance to share in chapel about peacemaking in the Qur'an. Later we sent a Somali woman who also had a positive experience and learned much that surprised her about Christians. For example, a Christian whose son had died said that he was angry at God. That was completely foreign to her. "How can you be angry at God? If he died, it's because God allowed it to happen. This is God's will."

At the same time, she told us about a priest who did not talk to her the first fifteen days because she was Muslim and he was afraid of her. After they met, he realized she was a nice person and apologized for his earlier attitude. That was interfaith bridge building, although our intention was simply to train somebody to be a peace facilitator. But when Muslims and Christians work in the same context, interesting and unexpected interfaith communication happens.

WHAT WE HAVE DONE,
WHAT WE HAVE LEARNED

It is hard to say what Mennonites have accomplished in Somalia, as Somalia is a place in which it is hard to measure anything. Somalia currently is in the throes of a civil war, within which what is done today may be undone tomorrow. Thus one must work in faith, believing that what is being done will bear fruit at some point. But we can be sure of one thing: a bridge has been built between Mennonites and Somalis—Mennonite people who are Christian and Somali people who are Muslim.

One of the sad things about the Somalia-Mennonite story is that while it is relatively well-known among Somalis, few Mennonites are aware of this history and these ongoing connections. As non-Mennonites, my husband and I have tried hard to make the story known among Mennonites because there are so few stories of a Muslim and a Christian people walking together through fifty years of history. Therefore to answer the question about what MCC and EMM have done and are doing today, we could simply say this: They have built bridges, and those bridges have allowed us to walk alongside Somalis during this very difficult time of their history.

Many lessons have been learned from the story. First, we have learned that it takes time to build bridges. To build bridges in an interfaith context, you need trust. Trust cannot be built in three months or even three years. Building bridges is the result of a long-term commitment to a particular group of people.

We have also learned that it takes risks to build bridges. Consider, for example, the events in spring of 2003 when U.S.-led forces invaded Iraq. An MCC worker named Kathleen, a single woman in her fifties with a ten-year-old daughter, was teaching at a nursing school in the most fundamentalist part of Somalia. When the war in Iraq started, all of the international NGOs in the region left because they feared a violent anti-Western reaction to the U.S.-led invasion. Mark, my husband, had a conversation with Kathleen to discuss whether or not she should leave. She told Mark that she would stay because her friends in the village had told her it was safe. Besides, she said, "I am two weeks behind in my teaching, and if I come out of the country, I will be even further behind."

When the international NGOs left, she stayed with her daughter. Kathleen was already known in her community as a woman who lived simply, who slept on the floor and cooked on a charcoal burner, but now she became known as the Mennonite woman who came and stayed with her daughter when everyone else left. This is another story which will be retold by the Somalis, added to the ones which have come before and kept the Mennonite name alive.

It takes risks to build bridges, because this can be life-threatening. But it is also risky because it leads to uncharted theological territories. In the 1960s, when the Mennonites decided not to close the schools, but to remain open and to allow Islam to be taught, they took a stand which left them open to criticism.

Finally, we have learned that an Anabaptist theology which insists on nonviolence is well-suited to deal with interfaith bridge building. Nonviolence means a refusal of any kind of evangelism that is aggressive or deceptive. I think the nonviolent stance helps to relate to people of another faith in a more respectful way. Moreover, because of the current global politics, to enter interfaith dialogue with Muslims, we must distance ourselves from any state or government policy which promotes war. To explain that peace is an integral part of our faith is the only way we can be credible.

Before closing, I want to address the issue of how to deal with Somalis or any Muslims who decide to be Christian. Conversion is a taboo issue in some circles. It is taboo for most Muslims, of course, because Islamic law places a heavy penalty on apostasy. It is also taboo, however, among some Christians who do not believe in the exclusivity and normativity of doctrinal claims about Jesus. While MCC is not a mission agency, it should be clear about what it believes about conversion, because it will be confronted with the question in areas in which MCC works alongside Muslims.

For example, at MCC-sponsored peace conferences in which different Somalia factions sought to draft a workable constitution, the drafts invariably stipulated clearly that the only religion to be allowed in the region would be Islam—not just that Islam would be the official religion, but that it would be the only one. While desiring peace for Somalis, how could we as Christians support such a process? Can we conceive of supporting both Somali peacemaking *and* the right of Christian Somalis to exist?

It is a great gift that Mennonites can relate so well to Muslim Somalis and partner with them on a myriad of projects, but what about their relationship with Somalis who decide or have decided to become Christians? The programmatic danger for MCC and EMM, in the Somali case, is not to refuse to partner with the Somali Muslims, which is a given. The key danger, rather, is that we might refuse to establish partnerships with the few Somali Christians, or that we might remain silent on the question of whether or not Somali Christians have a right to exist. How can we promote a spirit of tolerance in the peace effort we support?

To close, I would note the greatest challenge that the Somalia-Mennonite story faces today: its survival. Recruiting volunteers for Somalia because of the danger involved is a challenge, as North American risk-averse culture makes security a first priority. Some, meanwhile, might question ongoing Mennonite involvement in Somalia due to lack of measurable results. A risk-averse culture and an emphasis on quantifiable progress over relationship-building, then, are factors that could combine to threaten this miraculous relationship forged between Somalis and Mennonites. My plea to Mennonites is simple: Do not destroy the bridge that has been built over fifty years with significant sacrifice! The story, with God's grace, needs to go on!

NOTE

Mohamed Mohamed-Abid, *Histoire des Croyanies en Somalie* (Besançon: Annales Literéraires de l'Université de Besançon, 1992), 120.

Chapter 5

Interfaith Encounters in the Hindu Kingdom: Mennonites in Nepal

By Edgar Metzler

*W*hen Rudy Friesen from Manitoba arrived in Nepal in 1956, at age twenty, he could not have imagined that he would be the forerunner for nearly 150 Mennonites who would follow him over the next fifty years to serve in the world's only official Hindu kingdom. He transferred to Nepal from a year and a half of service in India. This was undoubtedly good preparation for working in a Hindu context, but Nepal was different, because, until a few years before Friesen's arrival, few foreigners had visited this small country. The first road into the capital was completed only the year Friesen arrived. Geographic and political isolation reinforced a strong cultural identity. Any change of religion from the state-sponsored Hinduism was forbidden by law.

Later that year, two volunteers serving under Mennonite Central Committee's PAX program for draft-age young men arrived. The next year Lena Graber, a missionary nurse working with the Mennonite Board of Missions (MBM) in India, transferred to Nepal to help develop a nursing school. Since those first pioneers, more than 100 Mennonite Central Committee

(MCC) workers have served in Nepal. Through MBM (and its successor agency, Mennonite Mission Network, or MMN), thirty-eight more have served. Some stayed for long terms, such as Miriam Krantz, a nutritionist, now a veteran of more than forty years.

Those early workers and those who followed arrived with the simple motive of serving in the name of Christ. Their service built bridges of friendship and collaboration between members of the dominant Hindu society on the one hand and the Christian expatriate workers on the other. Those bridges were essential for achieving the developmental goals for which visas were granted to outsiders.

As expatriate Christian workers became friends with their Nepali colleagues, they were rewarded with a fascinating and sometimes challenging introduction to new beliefs and behaviors. At the organizational level, Mennonites were challenged with the task of being part of a large Christian service agency trying to cooperate with a highly bureaucratic government cautious about foreign involvement and dedicated to preserving Hindu dominance. This chapter describes the nature of Mennonite interfaith encounters with Nepali society, with the government, and within the United Mission to Nepal (UMN), where Mennonites were only one part of a multifaceted decision-making process.

The structure of Mennonite service in Nepal is unique. There was and is no "MCC program" or "MBM/MMN program" separate from the United Mission to Nepal, an ecumenical coalition of forty church-related organizations from sixteen countries.[1] Eight mission agencies from Europe and North America established UMN in 1954, when the country first opened to the outside world. Other agencies soon joined, including MBM in 1957. MCC joined later, in 1974, although MCC had sent PAX volunteers earlier to serve under UMN. Representatives from MCC and MBM headquarters have actively participated on the UMN board, often serving on its executive committee. Mennonite engineers, doctors and other health professionals, educators, rural developers, administrators, and others with specific occupational and managerial skills have worked at every level of the organization, from remote village projects to headquarters leadership.

The government of Nepal initially invited UMN to start medical projects because the country had practically no social service infrastructure. UMN health services developed to include four hospitals, community health programs, mental health services, and nutrition outreach. UMN also established schools at all levels, including the country's first nursing school, the first girls' school, and the first technical school. Later UMN helped build the first private university. Agriculturists, foresters, veterinarians, and community development workers serving under UMN responded to needs in remote areas.

Unusual avenues of service for a church-related agency included technical training and the launching of private companies in which UMN's founding shares would eventually be transferred to the companies as they matured in technical and managerial competence. Many Mennonites worked in these companies, one of which became the major developer of hydropower plants. By the 1990s the UMN staff had grown to more than 200 expatriates with job-related visas (not including spouses and children) and 2,000 Nepali staff working in forty projects.

Why has this Christian mission and service organization engaged in such a large program of direct implementation of development projects? Because Nepal, emerging from a feudal economy as one of the least developed countries in the world, had almost no trained human resources to develop the services needed to meet basic human needs. From its inception, UMN hoped to transfer schools, hospitals, industries, and other development programs to local partners. That gradually happened, and in recent years the process has accelerated. Nepali organizations now implement most of the work begun by UMN.

Over the past five decades, MCC and MBM have been integral parts of UMN's governance. Both agencies contribute personnel to UMN's international team, where the identity of each worker's supporting organization holds less importance than the worker's solidarity within the larger coalition.

After Nepal's democratic revolution and the ratification of its new constitution in 1990, encounters between Nepali Hindus and members of other faiths became more open and sometimes more controversial. As Executive Director of UMN from 1990 to 1998, I had the opportunity to participate in some of these encounters. Together with my wife, Ethel Yake, whose psychotherapy practice in Nepal served Christians, Hindus, and Buddhists, I was jointly sponsored by MCC and MBM. As my survey of UMN work will show, Mennonites have been privileged to be a part of an innovative, if at times challenging and complicated, venture—a venture that has created and sustained bridges of interfaith friendship and collaboration.

THE NEPALI CONTEXT

To tell the story of the UMN experiment properly requires some knowledge of the Nepali context. Nepal is a small country, 500 miles long and 100 to 150 miles wide. The terrain moves in sharp contrast from a narrow strip of low, flat land along the Indian border to the Himalayan range along the northern border with Tibet. The massive mountain ranges in the north and the malarial jungles in the south played major parts in Nepal's almost total isolation from the rest of the world until the middle of the twentieth century.

The country contains a wide variety of ethnic groups and languages. Nearly half the population speaks a mother tongue other than the national language, Nepali. The census records twenty other languages, and linguists have found many more. These languages represent a diverse range of ethnic groups among half the population who identify their ethnicity as something other than Nepali. The 2001 census placed Nepal's population at twenty-three million. By 2006 the population had increased to an estimated twenty-eight million, giving Nepal one of the highest population growth rates in Asia.[2]

Nepal legalized the role of caste, a hierarchical division of society with Brahmans at the top, only in 1854.[3] Compared to India, caste principles may be somewhat muted in Nepal, but they continue to play a significant role in cultural, religious, and social affairs. Researchers estimate that although the main Brahman groups constitute only twenty-two percent of the population, they hold ninety-three percent of the higher civil service and political posts.

Until the eighteenth century, Nepal was a collection of dozens of small kingdoms with no established national boundaries. Prithvi Narayan Shah, considered father of the country, gradually conquered the territories of smaller kingdoms, finally overthrowing the most powerful kings located in the Kathmandu Valley in 1768. He declared himself king of the whole country, with borders about equivalent to the present state.

Nepal's mountains provide natural geographic barriers, one factor in the country's long isolation. Prithvi Narayan Shah also instituted a deliberate policy of maintaining closed borders. According to Nepal's leading historian, the late Rishikesh Shaha, the new king was strongly influenced by experiences in his youth with Western colonialism. Sent for a period of religious instruction to the holy city of Benares in northern India, he learned of the economic domination of the British East India Company and the torture-enforced conversions by Portuguese soldiers and priests on the Malabar Coast of southwest India. He determined that Nepal would not suffer the same fate.[4]

The policy of isolation lasted in various forms for almost two centuries. In the middle of the nineteenth century, the prime minister seized power from the king, and for the next hundred years his descendants ruled the country as a private fiefdom. In 1951, the king regained full power and opened the borders, at which point he began permitting limited entry of foreigners and foreign ideas. Indigenous demands for popular rule, meanwhile, were suppressed. The king introduced some measures of popular participation but retained monarchical control. He jailed opposition political leaders or exiled them to India.

In 1989, the major Nepali opposition party and a coalition of communist parties joined in planning a nonviolent campaign to bring parliamentary democracy to Nepal. The democratic revolution began February 1990. On April 9, late at night, King Birendra conceded his rule, but only after hundreds of deaths from the government's violent attempts to squelch the democratic movement. The country adopted a new constitution in November 1990, then held its first parliamentary elections in April 1991.

In a country with centuries of suffering under autocratic rulers, democracy has not proven to be the solution the revolution promised. The elderly idealistic leaders who spearheaded the movement succumbed to the temptations of power when they entered the government. In 1996, several communist politicians gave up on democracy and started an armed insurgency under the label of "Maoists." More than 13,000 persons have been killed in the ongoing conflict between the Royal Army and the Maoists. The king closed parliament in February 2004 and only reconvened it in May 2006.

No one knows how the conflict will be resolved, but the Maoist rebels recently agreed to a cease-fire and a return to electoral politics. Political instability, meanwhile, deepens the country's bleak economic realities. The United Nations rates Nepal as one of the poorest in Asia. A third of the country lives below the poverty level, according to a 2004 government estimate.

Government figures present Hinduism as the overwhelmingly dominant religion. The 2001 government census reported the religious composition of the country as 80 percent Hindu, 11 percent Buddhist, 4 percent Muslim, 0.45 percent Christian, and 4.6 percent other. These percentages translate into an estimated 103,500 Nepali Christians, an increase from the 1991 census figure of 47,600. The 1991 count may have been fairly accurate, but Nepal's Christian leaders claim the current number of Christians might be as high as 700,000. Buddhists also question the accuracy of the census. During the debate about the new constitution in 1990, Buddhists asserted that they formed 45 percent of the population and should thus not have to live under a Hindu state. That exaggerated number, in the context of the increasingly loud voices of fundamentalist Hindu elements, represented the Buddhist desire to claim their place in the new order promising increased religious freedom.

Relations between Hindus and Buddhists in Nepal had in the past always been amicable at the community level. One Nepali anthropologist told me that for many Nepalese the question, "Are you Hindu or Buddhist," would be puzzling. Many Nepalese revere both Hindu and Buddhist shrines. Many Hindu temples also have statues of the Buddha. Nepal never suffered the religious sectarian strife that has plagued India. Muslims, located mainly along the Indian border, have been a small enough minority that they have generally been tolerated, although in past centuries there had been an animus against the Muslims because of their conquest of India and the accompanying desecration of Hindu and Buddhist shrines.

Religion pervades all aspects of Nepali society. A longtime worker with UMN, Norma Kehrberg, summarizes the Nepali "mosaic of religions" with words that ring true to anyone who has lived among the people of Nepal: "The borrowing, blending, adapting and assimilating rituals and practices of different beliefs, create the composite of what can be called religion in Nepal. This rich mixture permeates all aspects of life—one's culture, family, work, and citizenship."[5]

The generally tolerant relations between Hindus and Buddhists have not always extended to Christianity. The first Christian representatives known to have entered Nepal were a small group of Capuchin Fathers who negotiated with the local kings in the Kathmandu Valley to maintain a small presence that lasted from 1715 to 1768.[6] Fearing Western intrusions as in India, the ruler of the new unified country asked the Fathers to leave.

For the next two centuries, the borders of Nepal remained closed to foreign influence. In the early 1950s, four Mar Thoma Christians from South India (related historically and theologically to the Syrian Orthodox Church) started a church in Kathmandu. Around the same time, the government allowed two foreign Christian organizations, the International Nepal Fellowship and the United Mission to Nepal, to start medical work in the country. Meanwhile, Nepali-speaking Christians from the Darjeeling area of India, just across the eastern border, moved into Nepal to plant gospel seeds that would bear fruit, surviving the hostile climate of the next three decades.

INTERFAITH ENCOUNTERS WITH THE GOVERNMENT

The 1962 constitution declared Nepal a Hindu state with the stipulation that the king must be Hindu. The constitution stated, "Every person may profess his own religion as handed down from ancient times and may practice it having regard to the traditions. Provided that no person shall be entitled to convert another person from one religion to another." The civil law that applied these provisions made clear their intent: "No person shall propagate Christianity, Islam, or any other faith so as to disturb the traditional religion of the Hindu community in Nepal or to convert any adherent of the Hindu religion to these faiths. Anyone attempting to do so shall be imprisoned for three years; where conversion has been effected, for six years."[7]

Persons jailed for converting were required upon release to revert to Hinduism. Foreigners accused of trying to convert Nepalese received severe penalties of fines and jail and were deported after release from prison. New Christians were jailed for having voluntarily changed their religion and for engaging in normal church activities. An Amnesty International report documented the government's harassment, torture, and "disappearance" of Christians.[8]

With the advent of democracy, Nepali Christians felt a new sense of freedom and enthusiastically used the opportunity to witness publicly to their faith in ways difficult or impossible before. The king announced his acceptance of the demands for democracy on April 9, 1990, Palm Sunday. Some Nepali Christian leaders proposed to the churches that Christians march through the main area of Kathmandu, past the palace, on Easter Sunday. Other leaders were cautious, but the march proceeded, with several hundred Christians carrying large signs celebrating the resurrection of Christ and calling for religious freedom. It was an exhilarating experience for believers who for years had been oppressed, worshiping secretly in homes and churches behind walls with no identifying signs.

A few weeks later, the euphoria of religious liberty rose to new heights as 2,000 Christians packed the largest auditorium in Kathmandu. Several of the senior democratic political leaders spoke at the meeting, promising religious liberty under the new constitution. In June 1990, only two months after the king conceded, the interim government dismissed more than 150 cases pending against Christians and released thirty-one prisoners serving jail sentences for religious reasons, thirty of them Christians, along with one Muslim.

The country's educated class vigorously debated the role of religion under democratic rule during summer 1990 as a new constitution was being drafted.[9] Fundamentalist Hindus, Buddhist clergy, and secular intellectuals contested the matter in the press. I had the opportunity for a lengthy conversation with the chair of the constitutional commission about matters of religious freedom. A high-ranking Buddhist monk published a stinging rebuke to a Hindu scholar who claimed that Buddhists were merely an accepted sect under the Hindu panoply of gods. On June 30, a demonstration of the Nepal Buddhist Organization brought over 10,000 marchers to the streets demanding a secular state. The palace, backed by Hindu organizations, pushed hard to retain the Hindu identity of the state in the new constitution. In the end the political parties compromised with the king, and the Hindu identity of the state remained.

The November 1990 constitution did improve the prospects for religious freedom, dropping the former prohibition against voluntary conversion. It also deleted the requirement that a person convicted of changing religion must return to Hinduism after punishment.

A subsequent 1992 law governing religious activities had positive and negative elements. The old law had prohibited anyone from "disturbing the rites of the Hindus." The new law made it illegal to "undermine *any* religious function." One member of parliament described this amendment as an attempt to stop blatant ridicule or defamation of other religions.

The fundamentalist Hindu influence resulted in retaining some of the old restrictions:

> No person shall propagate any religion in a manner likely to undermine another religion or convert anyone into another religion. In case he has only made an attempt to do so, he shall be punished with imprisonment for not more than three years. In case he has already converted anyone into another religion, he shall be punished with imprisonment for not more than six years. If he is a foreign national, he shall be deported from Nepal after completing such sentence.

However, the government made few arrests under the 1992 law. In two of these cases the charge was distributing Christian literature; several believers spent time in jail. Many persons converting to Christianity still face opposition from family and home communities and sometimes from local officials.

Although Nepali Christians enjoyed greater religious freedom, the legal situation for expatriate Christians working in Nepal remained the same. The government has never given visas for church-related work. The first American Jesuits to enter Nepal in 1951—the first one being Father Moran, whose mother came from a northern Indiana Mennonite family—received visas limiting them to educational work. To obtain visas, UMN workers needed qualifications for medical, educational, engineering, agricultural, or other professional and administrative areas.

The government of Nepal entered cautiously into relationships with a Christian service agency. The first brief agreement between the government and UMN, May 8, 1953, stated that the medical work being started would be "turned over to the government in five years," and that "The staff should be drawn from Nepali citizens as far as possible and they should be trained properly." The government soon realized that the country lacked enough trained Nepalese to carry the medical work forward. Nepal had almost no medical education until UMN established a nursing school.

The government omitted the five-year limit in the 1960 agreement. The new agreement reflected some government concern about the role of expatriates. It stipulated, "Members of the Mission during their stay in Nepal shall be subject to the laws of Nepal." More pointed was an added clause, "The members of the Mission shall confine their activities to the attachment [sic] of the objectives of the institution to which they are assigned and shall not engage in any extracurricular activities."

What were suspect "extracurricular activities?" The government was more specific in the 1969 agreement. Expatriates working with the Mission "shall not engage in any proselytizing and other activities which are outside the scope of their assigned work." The 1980 and 1985 agreements retained these restrictions. In November 1990, after the adoption of the constitution, the government added another specific restriction: expatriates "shall not engage in any proselytizing or political activities." The Foreign Ministry official negotiating that agreement suggested this was added out of concern about potential foreign influence on domestic politics.

The definition of proselytizing was ambiguous. Jonathan Lindell, UMN Executive Director in 1969 when the government first proposed this restriction, believed it was redundant. If this was meant, he wrote to the UMN Executive Committee, "to control our religious activities, they were already doing so in the clearest way by the earlier point which says that the Mission shall be subject to the laws and regulations of Nepal. There are clear and strong laws concerning religious activity and change. . . . I see no essential change here."

An opportunity to clarify the meaning of proselytizing arose in 1990, when the Secretary of Foreign Affairs working with us on the agreement proved to be very supportive of UMN. After agreeing on all the details of the agreement, he asked if there was any other issue UMN wanted considered. I mentioned that some ministries, including the Home Ministry, had delayed visas or project approvals because of allegations of proselytizing. I suggested that it would help UMN if the government could clarify the definition. He asked me to suggest a wording. Several days later he agreed to place a letter in the government files that defined proselytizing as "attempting conversion by coercion or offer of material inducement." The definition was quite acceptable and proved useful in discussions with government officials who occasionally confronted us with charges of proselytizing, none of which proved true.

In several situations I told government officials that if there was proof of any expatriate staff bribing or offering a job to anyone to become Christian, UMN would send the person home for violating our agreement with the government. It never happened, but the questions surfaced repeatedly. Authorities never explained some government actions adversely affecting UMN, but UMN suspected allegations of proselytizing had played a role.

In 2005, UMN's new agreement with the government for the first time came under the aegis of Nepal's Social Welfare Council. The council's protocol did not use the proselytizing language but stated the same concern another way. No organization, the agreement stipulated, may "get involved or allow the use of its means and resources, directly or indirectly, in activities relating to religious conversions which are prohibited by current law."

Although the narrative above indicates a persistent pattern of government suspicion of Western Christians, from Privithi Narayan Shah in the eighteenth century to the lawmakers in 1992, the United Mission to Nepal generally enjoyed cooperation and good relations with the government. The new democratically elected government in 1991 demonstrated a willingness to work with UMN. The prime minister met with the UMN Executive Director. At least six members of Parliament contacted UMN about possible projects in their districts. The Foreign Sec-

need definitions to work in agreement

retary came to a meeting of the UMN Board in November 1990 to sign a new five-year agreement.

The dramatic political developments in the spring and early summer of 2006 have greatly diminished the power of the Hindu king and moved Nepal toward becoming a secular state. Any difficulties UMN now experiences in securing agreements and visas probably have less to do with religious concerns and more with the government's desire for more control over international nongovernmental organizations and for assuring Nepali management of external resources, factors exacerbated by bureaucratic caution in a time of political uncertainty.

UMN's policy development over the last fifteen years pushed toward implementing the long-standing intention to evolve UMN projects into Nepali hands, emphasizing the development of Nepali capacity. UMN has moved steadily in this direction, transferring most of its projects to Nepali management. At the same time the government seems inclined toward reducing expatriate participation in development activities.

INTERFAITH ENCOUNTERS WITH THE SOCIETY

The work and presence of UMN have generally been appreciated by most elements of Nepali society. On several occasions I have heard government officials, including a prime minister, refer positively to the work of UMN and state that civil servants need more of the "missionary spirit." After the political changes in 1990, UMN could be more connected with and visible to the Nepali public. Invitations came to UMN to participate in various forums to present its perspective on development issues. *HIMAL* magazine, the foremost serious opinion journal in Nepal, in 1993 printed a long critical response I submitted to a major article on the history of Christianity in Nepal. This opened the door to many significant conversations.

The tragic crash in July 1992 of a Thai Airways flight trying to land at Kathmandu in stormy weather took the lives of 128 passengers (including the son of one UMN couple). The passengers came from many countries and represented many religions. A group representing the airline, the government, and the local diplomatic corps asked me, as Executive Director of UMN and an ordained minister, to lead the memorial service. The service

[handwritten margin note: coming together in tragedy]

included prayers and readings from the sacred texts of Buddhists, Hindus, Muslims, Jews, Zoroastrians, and both Catholics and Protestants. Prayers were offered in the name of Christ and New Testament Scriptures were read. Comments afterward expressed appreciation that Christians responded to this tragic situation in a spirit of service that built bridges to other faiths while clearly articulating their own faith through Scripture and prayer.

One element of Nepali society felt threatened by the presence of Christians, namely, the activist fundamentalist expression of Hinduism. Organizationally, this branch of Hinduism was represented by the World Hindu Federation (WHF), with headquarters in Kathmandu. Founded a quarter century ago, the WHF has been aligned with the fundamentalist anti-Muslim Hindu forces in India. In Nepal in the 1990s, the WHF became alarmed about the rapid expansion of Christianity, as Nepali believers freely shared their faith.

The WHF could not believe that anyone would change from the Hindu religion of his or her family and community without receiving some material advantage. So they charged that foreign Christians working with organizations such as UMN were out in the hills offering money or jobs in exchange for conversion to Christianity. Several times I met with the president of the WHF to discuss these charges, but he could not present any evidence.

On one occasion the WHF called a press conference and displayed a handwritten letter in Nepali script they had received from a secretary employed by a UMN project in the town of Pokhara. The letter claimed that the expatriate Christian project director had offered her bribes to become Christian. I immediately faxed the letter to the project leader, who showed it to the secretary. She was outraged, insisting it was a forgery, and demanded that the project leader take her to the district magistrate's office so she could swear out an affidavit that she had not written that letter. The WHF never publicly retracted the charge, but after that they seemed to back off from public statements and worked behind the scenes to influence government officials.

UMN expatriate Christians have lived and worked in many districts of Nepal, from the metropolitan capital to remote villages. Every place has offered opportunities to develop relationships with co-workers, neighbors, and friends of different religions. The religious nature of Nepali culture usually made con-

[handwritten at bottom: relationship]

versation about faith natural and appropriate. Many expatriates made efforts to enter sympathetically into the understandings and practices of their Nepali friends. They opened their homes for friendship, language lessons, non-formal education, and to teach handicrafts or other skills, especially for women. They demonstrated Christian values in personal life and project activities (for example, no caste distinctions were observed).

Through these natural human relationships, Nepalese in local communities became familiar with the Christian faith, and some wanted to make Jesus a part of their lives. Without proselytizing, as the government understood the term, a personal dynamic was at work, and in almost every place where UMN had a project, a small church emerged. The misconception in the law was that we could convert anyone. Only God can do that.

There were times and places where local political sensitivities to the Christian presence made relationships more challenging. But the overwhelmingly positive feelings almost all UMN workers had about their Nepali friendships testify to the possibilities of interfaith bridge building. For Christians committed to sharing Jesus in their life and work, the first step will be respect for the faith of others. Such respect is offered when faith is shared more through relationships than rational arguments.

INTERFAITH
ENCOUNTERS WITHIN THE MISSION

Almost from the beginning of UMN, the majority of the staff was Nepalese. Annual reports in the early years did not include the number of Nepali staff, although a 1970 report estimated 700 Nepali staff working with UMN. In 1987, the expatriate staff totaled 329 with 1,700 Nepali staff. By 1991, the foreign Christian staff numbered 231, a decline partly attributed to UMN's increased efforts to involve Nepali staff in more administrative and technical positions as more local qualified staff became available. By 1993, the expatriate number dropped to 174, and the number of Nepali staff rose to 2,000.

Most of UMN's Nepali staff is Hindu, along with some Buddhists. No employee records indicate religious affiliation. Estimates of the number of Christians among the staff of almost 2,000 ranged from five to ten percent.

UMN policies on employment clearly state that in regard to recruitment and promotion "There shall be no discrimination on the basis of race, sex, caste, or religion." But non-Christians had never been appointed to project leadership. For years there had been discussion about "Nepalization," the term used to describe the process and goal of involving more Nepalese staff in higher levels of management. One of the challenges was that few Christians had the training, expertise, and experience to lead large, technically advanced development projects. During the 1980s, there was increasing frustration, particularly on the part of some board members, that there was little progress in moving toward Nepalization.

In early 1991, a test case posed the challenge: What if we could not find a qualified Christian, expatriate or local, to lead one of the more than forty projects? And what if a qualified Nepali non-Christian was available?

The leader of the Health Services Department tried in vain to recruit a director for an important community health program. The department director explained his dilemma to me and his conviction that a qualified Nepali could be found, perhaps someone already working with UMN. Since the appointment of a non-Christian to project leadership was a departure from precedent, I presented the issue to the UMN Executive Committee, who took the following action at their meeting on April 25, 1991:

> Executive Committee affirms the identity of UMN as stated in the constitution. ("To minister to the needs of the people of Nepal in the name and spirit of Christ, and to make Christ known by word and life.") Since the Coordinating Committee (the seven members of the senior management team) has the responsibility to fulfill these purposes, it is essential that all members of this body subscribe to the organization's purposes and statement of faith. At all other levels, personnel must subscribe to the values that inform and shape the organization and its service.

The action implied that project directors could be non-Christian. But it set a new criterion for the quality of service of all staff, expatriate and Nepaliz: "personnel must subscribe to the values that inform and shape the organization and its service." But what were those values? There were certainly assumptions, but the values had never been articulated in a way that became the official stance of the organization.

During the following year, we initiated an organization-wide process, involving all projects and all staff, to develop a statement of values. The discernment process involving our diverse religious backgrounds became, for many of us, a significant interfaith bridge-building experience. I recall being amazed as I sat with a group of gardeners, watchmen, and maintenance workers spontaneously generating values they considered essential for UMN's success. At a later stage in the process, the task force working on the statement met in the headquarters conference room to survey the lists of values submitted by various project groups.

As the papers recording the suggestions were taped onto the walls, I noticed the value of forgiveness on several lists. I asked, "How can we include such a distinctly Christian value as forgiveness if we expect all staff to demonstrate these values?" Immediately, a Hindu staff representative responded, "This value would be crucial for Nepal where organizations often don't function well because people hold resentments and won't work together. If we make it one of our core values, teams will function better." The final draft follows:

THE UNITED MISSION TO NEPAL
A STATEMENT OF VALUES FOR UMN STAFF

Preface

The culture of an organization includes those values that determine how the organization works and behaves. The Christian commitments of those who sponsor UMN, and the personnel they send to Nepal, are clearly described in the UMN Constitution.

The following list of values describes behaviors we consider important for all Nepali and expatriate staff who represent and work for UMN. We recognize they are ideals, but we intend to be accountable for their expression in UMN, influencing our programming and the selection and development of staff.

Values

1. Equality: We value and respect each person without making unjust distinctions based on status, wealth, caste, religion, relationship, gender or ethnicity.

2. Special Concern for the Poor and Disadvantaged: We give special priority to the poor, the vulnerable, and the oppressed, and seek to change those social structures and attitudes which disadvantage them.

3. Love and Service: We seek to identify with people in their needs and aspirations, sharing with compassion our time and capability, doing whatever is necessary without considering any tasks too menial or belittling.

4. Forgiveness: We will be willing to acknowledge resentments, to forgive and seek reconciliation. We will seek to deal with conflict openly and positively.

5. Integrity: We seek to be truthful. We require honesty in handling goods and money and responsibility in fulfilling our duties.

6. Professional Competence: We desire to excel in our work, to improve our competence and to be models of efficient and humane methods of work. We expect to achieve demonstrable results.

7. Participation: We are committed to enabling people to share in the processes of decision-making that affect them, thereby empowering them to be more effective in improving their lives. In these interactions, we all give and we all receive, we all teach and we all learn.

8. Training: We are committed to the daily task of training others, to passing on our skills and demonstrating our values to individuals and to the nation as a whole.

9. Cultural Sensitivity: We seek to live and work in ways that are culturally sensitive and appropriate in a nation that has such a rich diversity of custom and tradition.

10. Environment: We value the conservation and enhancement of the environment, recognizing that all humans, animals, and plants exist in an intricate dependence upon each other and upon all that sustains them.

11. Identification with Nepal: We identify ourselves with this nation and its people: respecting its distinctiveness, sharing in its struggle for improvement, appreciating its achievements, and committing ourselves to promote its good.

not committing to some western ideal of democracy

committing to this country

What if I had to commit to shared values like these?

12. Humility: We seek to learn before we teach, recognizing that the diverse people of Nepal have lived in their hills, valleys, mountains, and plains for hundreds of years and have acquired skills, knowledge, and customs that the outsider must understand and appreciate to serve with them. (Adopted by UMN Board of Directors, November 29, 1992)

An earlier draft of values, generated by discussion at the annual meeting of expatriate workers, had explicit trinitarian theological language. In the final draft this was modified for two reasons. First, we wanted the values statement to be more than a general declaration of principles. We wanted a tool that would have practical application for every member of the staff, whether Christian, Hindu, or Buddhist. This meant the values needed to focus on desired observable behavior. Project workshops to explore the significance and application of the values statement provided opportunities to respond to questions regarding the source of inspiration and authority for these values. Christian staff could then share their understanding of God as the source of these values and Jesus as their model and embodiment.

A second reason for using nontheological language arose from our desire to be more transparent with the government and the public. The government always knew that churches from many countries sponsored UMN and that the workers they sent were Christian. But as far as I had been able to determine, UMN had never shared with the government the christological clarity of UMN's constitutional purpose statement: "to minister to the needs of the people of Nepal in the Name and Spirit of Christ and to make Christ known by word and life, thereby strengthening the universal Church in its total ministry."

In the more open religious atmosphere following 1990, I believed it might be possible to be more transparent about our identity. Sharing the values statement with government officials and representatives of the press proved to be a positive experience. The values statement gave job applicants and new employees a clear sense of the expectations of the organization. It provided a useful measure for performance reviews and clear criteria in the rare cases when disciplinary action was needed.

Values were at the heart of a book published in 1991, *Fatalism and Development*, by Nepal's senior anthropologist, Dor Bahadur

Bista. The book sparked controversy and considerable resentment from Kathmandu's high caste elite of political leaders and intellectuals. Bista, himself from a high caste family, perceived a stringent critique of Hindu hierarchical society and what he presented as a culture of fatalism. He contended that this combination was antithetical to development for the whole society. The challenge was how to replace those values. Bista agreed to discuss his book with a group of UMN workers because, he said with a wry smile, "You people profess to know something about values." He had analyzed the problem but despaired of the society finding a solution without "something like a moral and intellectual equivalent of what you call conversion."

Some members of the UMN Board of Directors questioned whether the values statement would dilute the distinctly Christian identity of UMN. The Board asked for further study and in 1994 approved a statement on "The Christian Identity of the United Mission to Nepal." The statement begins, "UMN is a Christian organization." It then describes six ways this identity is expressed and maintained.

First, by "What we believe." Here the amazing development was that the forty mission and service organizations from sixteen countries, representing a wide theological and ecclesiological spectrum, agreed to a summary of their beliefs. The faith statements of these organizations had been collated and resulted in this summary of "shared beliefs":

- that God is active in the world, offering salvation, reconciliation, and hope through Jesus Christ;
- that all Christians are called to participate in God's mission;
- that the goal of that mission is the extension of the kingdom of God which Jesus proclaimed;
- that the church is the community of those who join with Jesus in the ongoing ministry of sharing the kingdom through worship, proclamation, and service;
- that God has a special concern for the poor;
- that we witness to God's grace by both word and deed.

The second way of expressing identity was "What we do and how we do it." After describing the various ways UMN seeks to address human need, the importance of values is emphasized:

UMN's Christian identity is further verified when this work is performed with a standard of excellence and with compassion and values reflecting the life of Jesus. . . . Values emphasized by Jesus in his life and teachings are recognized as part of the Christian identity of UMN by the wider Nepali community.

The third means of expressing Christian identity was through "Our partnerships with other Christians." In the new era of religious openness, it was possible to discuss this more directly. The churches had not been founded by foreign missionaries and did not depend upon foreign resources for their strength. UMN had always tried to be supportive of the Nepali church and expatriate workers participated fully in local congregations without taking formal leadership roles. "UMN, as a mission, does not plant churches, but thanks God when churches emerge in response to the Christian witness of word and deed." The section concludes with an affirmation of policy that "UMN services are available to all people regardless of race, creed, caste, or nationality."

The fourth means of expressing Christian identity was "Christian witness and presence." This section, as well as other parts of the statement, represented a search for a holistic missiology that would be relevant to and respectful of the culture and also true to the gospel. "UMN believes Christian witness occurs wherever Christians live out their lives in conformity with the mind and spirit of Jesus." Everyone could agree with this statement of personal possibility. More problematic was the challenge to imagine how the large organizations UMN had established for implementing development work could express and maintain their Christian identity. The Board affirmed that "Institutions also can be a vehicle for expressing the Christian gospel, values, and partnership with the church."

Turning over UMN's work to Nepali ownership and management had been a goal from the beginning. But as UMN projects and institutions became larger and more complex, doubts arose whether Christian values and identity could be maintained. Although the Nepali church began to grow rapidly in the early 1990s, it was clear that there were not enough professionally and technically trained Nepali Christians to manage all the projects. The 1994 policy statement expressed the hopes that many had for the way to maintain Christian identity: "... we believe that more Nepali Christians will develop higher professional and technical skills and will be more able to contribute to the Christian presence and witness of these programs." These hopes are becoming reality as local organizations, including Christian agencies approved by the government, develop the capacity to manage many of the programs UMN began.

The 1994 statement affirmed UMN's vision "for increasing Nepali capacity for their own development." The board recognized that the implementation of this vision would result in a changed role for expatriate Christians, "a future in which the expatriate presence will increasingly be within Nepali structures enhancing Nepali capacity for development and transformation. Whatever the future, UMN desires, with God's help, to continue to be a Christian presence in the nation, as a light on the hill and the salt of the earth."

The uncertainty about the future identity of UMN work turned over to Nepali control elicited a variety of responses from expatriate staff and the board of directors. Some worried about the quality of service that would result, others about possible corruption and favoritism based on caste or family connections, others that the Christian identity of the projects would disappear, and others that opportunities for Christian expatriate service would diminish.

These concerns were not new, as UMN had from earliest days envisioned turning over its work to Nepali hands. The founders of UMN were conscious of their recent experience in India, where foreign mission organizations had developed large institutions and were discovering how problematic it was for the Indian churches to assume their operations. They didn't want to repeat that in the new work in Nepal. But large foreign-sponsored institutions and programs had developed in Nepal and now potentially competing goals emerged: should these programs be turned over to Nepali management or should they maintain their Christian identity? Could both be done at once?

There was no easy solution to this dilemma. In May 1996, the UMN board tried again to incorporate both concerns in a major policy statement, "Our Vision and Strategy into the Twenty-first Century." The holistic character of the long-standing mission statement was affirmed, "to minister to the needs of the people of Nepal in the Name and Spirit of Christ, and to make Christ known by word and life, thereby strengthening the universal church in its total ministry."

But in describing how this mission would be fulfilled, the focus moved from UMN as an organization to a vision for Nepal: "Individuals and communities will be able to secure their basic needs in a sustainable manner through participation in effective and self-reliant Nepali organizations, including Christian organizations." Achievement of this vision would require UMN to give "highest priority to developing the capacity of Nepali organizations."

Undergirding this strategy was the belief "that ultimately the work of development in Nepal must be carried out by Nepalis developing their own organizations, fitting to their realities, their understanding, and their capacities." UMN thus would phase "out of project ownership and direct implementation, while phasing in activities to support Nepali organizations."

This strategy has now been largely implemented. It does not resolve the dilemma of identity but reduces the scale. More time will be needed to evaluate how the Nepali people perceive UMN after its removal of itself from the large programs that had benefited the poor of Nepal. Almost everyone agreed that the strategic direction was right but the challenge of Christian identity in the Hindu kingdom still confronts UMN workers in the smaller community-based programs now being established.

Meanwhile the growing church takes a larger role in responding to the needs of the country. As the government registers Christian NGOs, MCC and other international church organizations can second workers directly to them. Some church leaders also see the opportunity for the church to strengthen its witness by addressing issues of peace and justice. An organization formed for this purpose, Christian Efforts for Peace, Justice, and Reconciliation, has taken up issues of human rights and the conflict between the Maoist insurgency and the government.

The devastating impact of the Maoists has motivated leaders of several religious groups to join together to work for peace. One of the Christians involved reported that

The interreligious Committee is maturing steadily and

raising its voice very clearly for peace and justice and a negotiated settlement of the ongoing conflict. It is interesting
to note that Christians became the first to express concerns
over the deteriorating security and human rights situation
and to come up with a clear position on the whole situation
in the country. It is furthermore interesting that Christians,
a small minority not even officially recognized by the state
and major religious groups, became the leader in initiating
interreligious dialogue, cooperation, and understanding
which has reached a new height.[10]

Not all Nepali or expatriate Christians support this approach, but efforts of Nepali Christians to enter the interreligious arena with a clear Christian identity to further peace and
justice deserves the support of MCC. UMN priorities now include support for conflict resolution—an experienced conflict
resolution practitioner who has worked for many years with
MCC in Northern Ireland has taken on this new assignment. The
largest Nepali Christian NGO, Human Development and Community Services, which has taken on some UMN programs, also
addresses peace and justice issues.

Mennonites working in Nepal did not consciously employ
the interfaith bridge-building metaphor, as currently used by
MCC, but bridge building could describe what they were doing
as they developed significant relationships with people whose
culture and religious orientation differed profoundly from
theirs. The medium of exchange was not ideological persuasion
or theological debate but respect for others and desire to serve in
the name of Christ. The MCC Peace Committee suggests three
guidelines for interfaith bridge building:

1. Communicate as clearly as possible that we start
from the Christian claim that Christ is the light of the world;
2. Engage in interfaith partnerships both to accomplish
tasks together and to interact with the Other.
3. Desire . . . everyone to come to see their lives in light
of the gracious judgment of the cross, so that we may grow
together into the future human community that Jesus
made possible.[11]

The third point continues with the reminder that Western
Christians "carry implicit and explicit power into many of these

relationships. Exclusive claims must always be expressed with vulnerability. . . ."

As a lens through which to view the Nepal experience, these three guidelines highlight the challenge of being a Christian presence in a predominantly Hindu country. At the personal level, most UMN workers related to their friends, colleagues, and neighbors of other religions within the framework suggested by the guidelines, with a few exceptions at either end of the theological spectrum represented in UMN. At the organizational level, a lowkey (usually) but persistent fundamentalist Hindu voice in some quarters of public life at times strained UMN's generally collaborative relations with the government.

MCC advocates a "diaconal" approach to interfaith bridge building—through service, the approach followed by Mennonites since Rudy Friesen joined UMN in 1956. That approach correlates with UMN's purpose, "to minister to the needs of the people of Nepal in the name and spirit of Christ and to make Christ known by word and life." Restrictions on sharing the "Word" publicly did not prevent sharing in personal relationships. The witness of the "life" was manifest in service to others and the character of the server.

In North America, the artificial dichotomy of word and deed, evangelism and service, has impeded our embrace of a fully biblical holistic ministry. But in Nepal, appointees of both the service agency (MCC) and the mission agency (MBM) lived and worked together in ways that exemplified an integration of service and witness. There has been surprisingly little refection by Mennonites on the missiological significance of their extensive experience in service.[12]

A thoughtful Nepal government official I learned to know was Dr. Simkadda, director of the agency coordinating nongovernmental organizations. While studying for his doctorate in Florida, he and his family became close friends of neighbors who were retired Lutheran missionaries. They had served forty years at a remote mission outpost in Africa. Simkadda was deeply moved by this example of self-sacrificing service. He told me that he was gathering materials to write a book on the various motivations for service in the religions present in Nepal.[13] He asked for materials emerging from the Christian perspective.

When I gave him a box of papers and books on the subject, he put this question to me: "Where do Christians get this strong sense of duty to serve others?"

I replied instantly, and I felt the words were put on my lips, "It is not a sense of duty, Dr. Simkadda, but a strong sense of gratitude to God."

NOTES

1. Recently several Nepali Christian nongovernmental organizations gained government recognition. This allows foreign organizations to second limited personnel directly to them. MCC has made one such secondment.

2. Ministry of Population and Environment website: www.mope. gov.np/population.

3. Dor Bahadur Bista, *Fatalism and Development* (Calcutta: Orient Longman, 1991), 58.

4. Conversation with Rishekish Shaha in Kathmandu (Nov. 1992).

5. Norma Kehrberg, *The Cross in the Land of the Khukur* (Kathmandu: Ekta Books, 2000), 86.

6. For a fascinating account of these pioneers, see Jonathan Lindell, *Nepal and the Gospel of God* (Kathmandu: United Mission to Nepal and Pilgrim Book House, reprint ed., 1997). See especially chapter one, "Men in Beards, Hoods, and Robes," 1-37.

7. Muluki Ain, trans. Ramesh Khatry (Kathmandu: Law Books Publishing Committee, 1986), 241

8. Amnesty International, *Nepal: A Pattern of Human Rights Violation* (London: Amnesty International, 1987).

9. Michael Hutt, *Nepal in the Nineties* (London: Oxford University Press, London, 1994). See chapter 3, "Drafting the New Constitution."

10. Letter from K. B. Rokaya (Feb. 3, 2006).

11. *MCC Peace Office Newsletter* 35/4 (Oct.-Dec. 2005), 12.

12. Reflections on holistic ministry and relations with peoples of other faiths can be found in C. Norman Kraus, *An Intrusive Gospel? Christian Mission in the Postmodern World* (Downers Grove, Ill.; InterVarsity Press, 1998). A case study of the United Mission to Nepal is found in *Serving with the Poor in Asia: Case Studies in Holistic Ministry*, ed. Tetsunao Yamamori, Bryant L. Myers, and David Conner (Monrovia, Calif.: MARC Publications, 1995), ch. 1. For a brief personal reflection on her experience in Nepal by a former MBM appointee, see Margaret Entz Spare, *Doing the Gospel in Nepal*, Mission Insight Number 3 (Elkhart, Ind.: Mennonite Mission Network, 1999).

13. That book never materialized, but an excellent presentation of the philosophy of service and call to service in Hinduism, Buddhism, Judaism, Christianity, and Islam can be found in *Visions of Service*, ed. Linda A Chisholm (New York: The International Partnership for Service-Learning and Leadership, 2004).

Chapter 6

Interfaith Bridge Building, Peacebuilding, and Development: Learnings from Palestine-Israel

Alain Epp Weaver

*I*n 1998, Mennonite Central Committee (MCC) placed a service worker with the Al-Salah Islamic Society in the Gaza Strip. Al-Salah is a charitable society that operates kindergartens, youth clubs, and women's centers for income generation projects such as sewing and knitting. While not officially affiliated with Hamas or Islamic Jihad, Al-Salah's leadership comes from those who would be normally described as "Islamist" or "fundamentalist." In 1995-1996, my wife Sonia and I were asked to explore programmatic opportunities for MCC in the Gaza Strip. We knew that the MCC Middle East program at the time had placed an emphasis on developing connections with Muslim organizations, so when we became acquainted with Al-Salah late in our one year in Gaza, we asked about potential interest in a service worker to teach English to college students.

One year later, this connection resulted in James Wheeler being placed by MCC to offer adult English as a Second Language courses to young men out of Al-Salah's main office in the town of Deir el-Balah. At the same time, James and his wife Linda Herr served as MCC's program coordinators for the Gaza Strip.

Through the placement, James and Linda forged many friendships with families in Gaza's refugee camps. The placement was abruptly terminated, however, after Al-Salah leaders saw an imam on a Palestinian TV station from Hebron denounce the "Mennonite" school in Hebron as a place where Muslim children were being proselytized. This "Mennonite" school was the Arab Evangelical School in Hebron. Founded by MCC in 1952, operated by MCC until 1966, and led by Ada and Ida Stolzfus until 1988, the school—today administered by a Christian organization in Oklahoma—is still called the "Mennonite" school by many average Hebronites.

While MCC had had no administrative oversight or responsibility for the school since 1966, MCC still found itself linked to the school in the popular memory. This linkage had repercussions for the MCC Gaza program. "We know you're not trying to convert us," Al-Salah's leaders told Wheeler. "But if there would be even one mistake, our organization would be finished." Thus did a fascinating experiment end.

One wonders if MCC would, in our post-9-11 environment, engage in a partnership with Al-Salah, a group that, while independent of political affiliation, attracted its share of volunteers and workers sympathetic to Islamist political movements that would routinely be described as "terrorist." To what extent will we police ourselves in our interfaith bridge-building activities out of fear of being branded as on the wrong side of the "global war on terror"?

MCC IN PALESTINE-ISRAEL: A RICH HISTORY

MCC was one of the first foreign aid agencies to begin work in Palestine-Israel. MCC has worked alongside Palestinians since 1949. That was when MCC began to respond to the Palestinian refugee crisis, first through material aid distributions and other work in and around the refugee camps surrounding Jericho and later in the 1950s and 1960s through the establishment of self-help projects for women (specifically, the marketing of Palestinian needlework) and the founding of Christian schools in Hebron and Beit Jala. During the 1970s and the first part of the 1980s, MCC operated a rural development unit, helping Palestinian farmers throughout the occupied West Bank bring more land into cultivation with an eye to protecting it from confiscation by the Israeli military authorities. Also in the 1970s, following Israel's occupation of East Jerusalem, the West Bank, and the Gaza Strip, MCC began to look for ways to promote nonviolence and a just and durable peace for Palestinians and Israelis.

In the late 1980s, with the rapid growth of Palestinian civil society institutions, MCC program began to shift from MCC implementing its own projects to MCC supporting Palestinian initiatives in agricultural and women's development, early childhood education, and peacebuilding. More recently, MCC also began to work in direct partnership with Israeli peacebuilding organizations. Today MCC's work in Palestine-Israel clusters around three areas: assisting Palestinian farmers maximize scarce water resources; supporting the diaconal outreach of the Palestinian churches; and joining Palestinian and Israeli peacebuilding initiatives.

To what extent can MCC's development and peacebuilding work be described as interfaith bridge building? In the following pages I will provide brief sketches of select MCC projects, past and present, asking to what extent they should be understood as projects designed to nurture connections across religious borders.

Supporting Christian education

The Latin Patriarchate School of Zababdeh is a Roman Catholic K-12 school in the northern West Bank with a student body of 600. Two-thirds of the students come from Christian families (Orthodox, Greek Catholic, Roman Catholic, Anglican) in Zababdeh, while one-third are Muslims from the surrounding towns and villages, particularly but not exclusively from the secularized professional class in Jenin. Most of the teachers at the school are Christian, but there are also some Muslim instructors. The headmaster is the village's parish priest. MCC supports the school through a Global Family institutional sponsorship grant, a grant used to provide scholarships to low-income students and upgrade to the school's library and language lab facilities. Several MCC service workers have taught English at the school. The school headmaster describes the school as a place where lifelong friendships are forged between Christian and Muslim youth.

Refugee advocacy

MCC supports two organizations, one Palestinian and one Israeli, working for durable solutions for Palestinian refugees. The Palestinian organization is the Badil Resource Center for Residency and Refugee Rights. Badil produced, with MCC help, a Hebrew-language information packet aimed at Israeli Jewish audiences discussing Palestinian refugee return and compensation as vital components of any durable peace agreement. Badil in turn introduced MCC to the Zochrot Association, an Israeli organization which describes itself as dedicated to remembering the Palestinian refugee catastrophe, the *Nakba*, in Hebrew.

With MCC support, Zochrot organizes visits by Israeli Jews to the sites of destroyed Palestinian villages from 1948 inside Israel. Amid the ruins and remains of the destroyed locales, tour participants hear from displaced Palestinians about the village's history and about its demolition by Zionist forces. Zochrot has also helped the first ever dialogue workshops between internally displaced Palestinians on the one hand and members of an Israeli Jewish community built partly on the land of these internal refugees on the other. Badil and Zochrot conduct joint activities and share a common, rights-based approach to the Palestinian refugee case. Both Badil and Zochrot describe themselves as secular organizations.

Assisting the work of Christian social service agencies

The East Jerusalem YMCA is a Palestinian Christian organization operating a variety of social services throughout the occupied West Bank and East Jerusalem. The YMCA, which is institutionally tied to the Anglican church in Jerusalem and has an all-Christian governing board, employs both Christians and Muslims in its programs promoting women's development and the integration of persons with disabilities into Palestinian society. MCC supports these programs with annual financial grants. Nader Abu Amsheh, the director of the YMCA's Rehabilitation

Program for persons with disabilities, is a Palestinian Christian from Beit Jala who attends the local Baptist church. He describes the work of the East Jerusalem YMCA as part of the Palestinian church's diaconal witness within and to the wider society.

Palestinian liberation theology

The Sabeel Ecumenical Liberation Theology Center, a Palestinian Christian organization based in Jerusalem, arranges workshops for Christian clergy and Muslim scholars to share reflections with each other about particular topics (e.g., sacrifice); hosts an *iftaar* at which Palestinians and Muslims break the Ramadan fast together; and organizes tours for Muslim and Christian youth leaders of each other's holy sites.

MCC WORK IN PALESTINE-ISRAEL: IS IT INTERFAITH BRIDGE BUILDING?

Which of the examples described above—and many more, from Palestine and other parts of the Middle East, could easily be added—represent what MCC wishes to do under the rubric of "interfaith bridge building?" To be considered an example of bridge building, is it enough for a project to bring together persons from different religious backgrounds? Or is something more intended? Is interfaith bridge building to be the primary purpose of the project, or is it a beneficial byproduct?

Consider Christian schools in the Middle East, like the Catholic school in Zababdeh. Such schools have arguably done more than anything to foster positive relations between Christian and Muslim communities in the Middle East. Through Christian schools and through social service programs like those carried out by the East Jerusalem YMCA, a variety of church and church-related organizations in the Middle East make a diaconal witness within their wider societies. This witness consists at least in part of an embodied testimony to the reality that God's love reaches out to all and that God is at work outside the walls of the church, such as when a Palestinian Muslim trainer for the YMCA's Women's Training Program gives rural and refugee women skills they can use to take greater charge of their lives.

It isn't accurate, however, to portray the social service and development programs of church-related groups like the YMCA or the activities of Christian schools in the Middle East as primarily about interfaith bridge building. They're first and foremost about helping rural women gain greater financial control over their lives, improving accessibility for persons with disabilities, or providing a high-quality education. These projects might in the course of their implementation also build bridges of understanding and friendship between persons from different religious backgrounds, but they weren't started with the express purpose of building such bridges.

Another question—do our partner organizations have to be self-consciously religious for a project to qualify as an interfaith bridge-building effort? By supporting Badil and Zochrot, MCC is helping to build bridges between Palestinian Arab and Israeli Jewish communities. Yet both Badil and Zochrot are explicitly secular organizations that, while not hostile to religious organizations such as MCC, do not understand their work in religious terms. Zochrot and Badil are laying the groundwork required for any future reconciliation between Palestinians and Israeli Jews. By grappling with the past, by publicly acknowledging the massive dispossessions of hundreds of thousands of Palestinians in 1948, and by seeking to correct the ways in which Palestinian history has been erased from the Israeli landscape since 1948, Zochrot and Badil point Palestinians and Israeli Jews toward reconciliation.

Suhair Hasanian, a Palestinian refugee from the Palestinian town of Al-Majdal, now the Israeli city of Ashkelon, relates growing up on stories about how her parents and grandparents had been expelled from the city. Joining Israeli Jews from Zochrot on a trip back to Majdal, she says, "changed something for me." The trip, according to Suhair, was "a consolation, and consolation is a lot." Aya Kanyuk, an Israeli Jewish woman who has participated in Zochrot trips to destroyed villages, argues that "The need to acknowledge the suffering of the Other, to give him a name and a place, is not dangerous, but the opposite"— without speaking the truth about the past no reconciliation can be possible.

Speaking the truth, healing of memories, reconciliation. Like the Truth and Reconciliation Commission in South Africa realized, we're dealing here with profoundly religious concepts. But Zochrot and Badil don't describe the type of work they do as re-

ligious, so it would appear odd to try to fit this under an interfaith bridge-building rubric. Perhaps in the work of Badil and
Zochrot we have what Karl Barth called a "secular parable of the
kingdom," an embodiment outside the walls of the church of
God's reconciling Spirit in action. We can enthusiastically celebrate such parables, of course, without feeling the need to give
the "interfaith" label to all such bridge-building activities.

The ambiguity in this case arises in part because of the fact
that one of the parties with whom bridges are being built, the Israeli Jewish party, represents a religious community that simul-
taneously understands itself as a nation. Thus an exercise in interethnic or binational bridge building in the Palestinian-Israeli
context will inevitably include religion in the mix. The example
of Badil and Zochrot should also raise for us the question of the
complicated relationship between religious faiths and secular
ideologies—or should we say secular faiths?

For certain administrative matters—such as establishing criteria for how to use certain types of funds—it might make sense
to develop a restrictive definition of what counts as an interfaith
bridge-building project. However, this should not stop us from
reflecting on ways this new key initiative can spur us institutionally to think about innovative ways to present some of our existing programs. Thus, for example, MCC's support for the Latin
Patriarchate School in Zababdeh might not have started out of a
desire to help foster friendships and connections between Palestinian Muslims and Palestinian Christians. Having interfaith
bridge building as an institution-wide focus, however, pushes
us to recognize ways in which our current involvements are already strengthening the bonds of friendship and understanding
between persons from different religious backgrounds.

This in turn can and should lead us to think of innovative
ways to present these programs to our supporting constituencies in North America. Describing to Mennonite and Brethren in
Christ supporters in North America how a school like the Latin
Patriarchate School of Zababdeh or how the programs of the
East Jerusalem YMCA bring together Christians and Muslims in
joint endeavors, nurturing life-long friendships in the process,
provides a counter-narrative to the increasingly common narrative that assumes Christians and Muslims are inevitably and
necessarily in conflict with one another. Simply narrating how in

the course of normal, everyday life Christians and Muslims in Palestine, or in other parts of the Middle East, live together in friendship and trust deconstructs simplistic assumptions about a "clash of civilizations," assumptions that in Christianity and Islam we are dealing with inevitably warring essences.

MCC, THE CHURCHES OF THE MIDDLE EAST, AND INTERFAITH BRIDGE BUILDING

I began by describing some MCC Palestine project involvements to help us think through what we mean by interfaith bridge building. Perhaps, however, this was not a basic enough place to start our reflections. More basic is the question of what MCC's partners will think of having interfaith bridge building as an MCC key initiative. Do MCC's partners in peacebuilding work see interfaith bridge building as something warranting sustained attention? Do the churches to which we seek in some fashion to be accountable consider it a priority?

In the Middle East the answers would vary from country to country and sometimes within a country. For example, in Egypt various communal conflicts in different parts of the country have taken on a religious dimension, and Christians feel more acutely threatened by certain types of Islamism. There Christians will probably identify bridge building with Muslims to be a higher priority than, say, Christians in Palestine, Jordan, or Syria. In countries like Lebanon and Iraq where religious divisions have joined ethnic, national, and class divisions as catalysts to bloody conflicts, projects dedicated to connecting people across religious lines might well be welcome. Or they might be viewed with suspicion, the suspicion being that any project focusing on religious difference and division, even if the project's stated goal is to bridge those differences, will inevitably reinforce those divisions.

In the Palestinian context, for example, I can imagine that if MCC announces that it wishes to encourage projects that strengthen bonds between Christians and Muslims, the reaction of some of our partners will be critical. Palestinian Christians and Muslims are brothers and sisters, members of one nation, there are no differences to bridge, the argument would go. The very presumption that there are differences to bridge means, one might argue, the external construction of those differences.

Such a response points to something we need to keep in mind, namely that identities are always multiple and under negotiation. Being "Christian" in the Middle East—or anywhere in the world—doesn't exhaust one's identity: national identities, regional identities, educational and class factors all shape people's understandings of who they are. How individuals and groups negotiate these multiple strands of identity vary dramatically across time and place.

It's important to recognize that such identities aren't static, but are rather dynamic, always under construction. Part of the shifting nature of identity in the Middle East over the past century has been the forging of new national identities. Arab Christians have been at the forefront of the construction of national identities, be they pan-Arab nationalisms or more regional nationalisms, such as Palestinian nationalism.

Here is one way this plays out in daily life. In April 2004, I was waiting at a checkpoint with Father Aktham Hijazin, a Roman Catholic priest from Jordan who was then serving as the priest in the northern West Bank village of Zababdeh. It was raining. Fr. Aktham and I were getting wet as we tried to convince the soldiers that we should in fact be allowed to pass. As we waited for the soldiers to consult with their superiors (at least that's what they said they were doing), Father Aktham taught me the words to a Lebanese song that went like this: *Nahna mish irhabiyya, nahna sha'b al-hurriya; mislem wa-masihiye, nahna watan al-'arabiya* ("We are not terrorists, we are the people of freedom; Muslims and Christians, we are the Arab nation.")

The sentiments of this song, the inscription of Christian and Muslim identities within a pan-Arab or national identity, are ones heard quite frequently from Christians and Muslims in the Levant (Jordan, Palestine, Syria, and Lebanon), both publicly and in private. At the same time, this discourse stands in tension with more hostile appraisals of the religious Other. A Catholic priest with whom we worked in Zababdeh, and who now serves the parish in Gaza, routinely told us that there was no difference between Christians and Muslims. This priest is often called on to speak at political rallies. There he weaves Christian and Islamic references into a Palestinian national narrative. This same priest, however, once angrily described Islam to me as a "Satanic" religion—this after Christian and Muslim youth in Zababdeh had gotten into a street fight over claims that Muslim youth had made inappropriate comments to a Christian girl.

It might be natural to assume that one of these discourses is the "real" discourse and the other an affectation, but such an assumption is unwarranted. We shouldn't assume idyllically harmonious relations, nor should we assume relations of unmitigated conflict. Reality is messy and complicated, and how people construct their own identities and understand themselves in relation to others will always be matters under negotiation.

We must avoid essentializing moves built on the assumption that the "West," "Islam," "Christianity" and other such terms denote homogenous, static entities rather than dynamic and contested identities. Assuming that religions and religious identities are static and homogenous, after all, is the defining move of those (be they Christian or Muslim, from East or West) who want to convince us a "clash of civilizations" is inevitable.

Some of the dynamics that help to shape Christian-Muslim relations in the Middle East include memories of the Crusades and their violence against not only Muslims but also Eastern Christians; Western Christian complicity in the colonialism of the late nineteenth and early twentieth centuries; Western Christian support for Zionism; and the widespread reporting of disparaging comments about Islam made by various Western Christian leaders, such as Franklin Graham. Christians in the Middle East sometimes find themselves facing guilt by association for the actions and words of their Western co-religionists.

The fact that the impact of Western Christianity in the Middle East has been and continues to be negative in many ways should reinforce our commitment to be accountable to Middle Eastern Christians in relation to any proposed interfaith bridge-building efforts in the region. I therefore end these reflections by highlighting three implications being accountable to the church in the Middle East should have for how MCC approaches the task of interfaith bridge building.

The first implication is that we should be skeptical about applying the interfaith lens to the Palestinian-Israeli conflict. Many Israeli leaders wish to present the conflict as a religious one, part of a broader "clash of civilizations" or of the "Global War on Terror." I do not wish to deny that both Palestinians (Christian and Muslim) and Israeli Jews deploy religious discourse to justify violence. That said, a strong argument can be made that the Palestinian-Israeli conflict is not a Jewish-Muslim conflict but is best understood as a conflict between, on the one hand, a settler-colonial movement, Zionism, that seeks to extend control over particular territory, and on the other hand the indigenous population resisting such control.

That colonial movements use religious arguments to justify their claims to particular parcels of land and their control over particular peoples is nothing new, of course; neither is the fact that anti-colonialist insurgents use religious rhetoric to mobilize and justify resisting colonial practice. Even the most secular Zionists make implicit religious appeals alongside secular arguments for why the Jewish "nation" should rightfully control Palestine; even secular factions of the Palestine Liberation Organization rally followers with emotional, religiously based appeals to liberate Jerusalem. However, to view the Palestinian-Israeli conflict in primarily religious terms is to lose sight of the military and bureaucratic forms of power through which the Israeli regime extends control over land and people.

Too many initiatives carried out under the interfaith rubric serve to obscure these realities of power. The churches in Palestine call fellow Christians in Europe and North America to awareness of ways in which Israeli colonial practices dispossess Palestinian Christians (as well as Muslims) and, by crippling the Palestinian economy, threaten the church's existence in Palestine. This threat becomes acute as more and more Palestinian Christians emigrate, seeking to make a livelihood in the West.

A second implication of being accountable to Middle Eastern churches is that we will join Middle Eastern Christians in being unapologetic in our confession that Jesus Christ is Lord. We need to be clear among ourselves and with our supporting churches that we engage in interfaith bridge building *because*, not in spite, of our christological convictions. Our confession that Jesus Christ is Lord, that he is the way, the truth, and the life, that all salvation comes through him, should not serve as a stumbling block to forging alliances with those who do not name his name. Our confession should not prevent our cultivating openness to learning about God from those outside the church.

One temptation in any interfaith activity is to shy away from our particular confessions, to search for some neutral language to describe our faith convictions. But such a search is doomed from the start, for there is no neutral ground to be found. The bridge-building metaphor is problematic if it leads us to think of persons of differing faith convictions coming together at a neutral location. We need to expect, and be unapologetic about the fact, that people from different faiths will name the truths they discover in interfaith collaboration according to their own faith convictions. We should engage in interfaith bridge building not out of a low view of Jesus, according to which Jesus is one light among many others, but out of a high view of Jesus. To deny that there is truth to be found outside of the church, to deny the value of fostering friendships and collaboration among persons of different faiths, is to have too low a Christology.

Finally, a commitment to being accountable to the church in the Middle East in regard to interfaith bridge-building efforts should remind us of the continued importance of ecumenical work. In Egypt and in Syria, MCC has close partnerships with the Coptic Orthodox and Syrian Orthodox churches, respectively. Yet these are churches from which Mennonites, heirs to the radical Reformation, are estranged. The same could be said for the Roman Catholic and Chaldean Catholic institutions with which we work.

The decision by MCC and the Mennonite mission boards not to try to plant Mennonite churches in the Middle East has been, to my mind, a missiologically sound one: the last thing the church's witness to Jesus in the Middle East needs is more fracturing and splintering of Christ's body. Accompanying the churches of the Middle East, supporting them in their witness, is an exciting missiological adventure. Such ministries of accompaniment should be carried out in a vulnerable spirit, one in which we open ourselves to ecclesiological challenge.

Just as we should not be content with a pluralistic attitude in interfaith matters, our commitment to ecumenical partnership should not be driven by an embrace of denominational pluralism. Our partnerships with Roman Catholic and various Orthodox churches, all of which make strong ecclesiological claims about being the true church, present us with an opportunity to reflect on why we as Mennonite and Brethren in Christ communions remain separate, out of communion, with these churches.

Building ecumenical bridges through cooperation in the church's diaconal service to the wider society has been and should continue to be a defining characteristic of MCC's presence in the Middle East. But convergence in service ministries should not obscure ongoing doctrinal divergences. While we can and should affirm our common identity as Christians, the fact that we cannot share in the Eucharistic feast with many of our partners should remind us that the religious Other is often our Christian sister or brother. At least in the Middle East, then, building ecumenical bridges will be an indispensable part of what it means to be engaged in interfaith bridge building.

Chapter 7

A Dialogue of Civilizations: The Encounter of Iranian Shi'ites and North American Mennonites

Roy Hange

*W*hat does a "dialogue of civilizations" look like? In a famous speech broadcast on CNN in 1997, Muhammed Khatami, then president of Iran, called for a dialogue of civilizations instead of a clash of civilizations.

Humanity has explored earth and space and found much to fascinate. The unexplored frontiers in our world today, however, are more relational. The quality of our encounters along those frontiers could determine the future of humanity—politically, economically, and religiously. One such encounter is occurring between Iranian Shi'ite Muslims and North American Mennonite Christians, a student exchange helped by Mennonite Central Committee (MCC) and the Imam Khomeini Education and Research Institute (IKERI). This encounter has produced friendships, laughter, and even tears at times—all while acknowledging profound differences.

Through this program, Christians study and teach in Qom, Iran, while Shi'ite students study in Toronto. Matthew Pierce, who spent two years in Qom through the program, notes how life in Iran has opened up doors of mutual exchange and understanding:

> Advocates of dialogue often focus on conferences, books, articles, committees, etc. But in my experience, the most profound moments of dialogue have been unplanned and come out of the friendships that are formed naturally while living among Muslims. In a most ordinary flow of events, our neighbor invited us for dinner one night last year, and while there I met one of his friends, Sayyid Ata Anzali, who in turn invited us for dinner at his house the following week. We were quick to become friends, sharing interests in theology, the study of other religions, and goals of academic careers. Ata is a Sayyid. This means he is a descendant of Muhammad, the final prophet of Islam. Each week we meet together. We read the Bible together, we read the Qur'an together, and we have great conversations. The moments are rich, and they give me hope for the future of dialogue between Muslims and Christians.[1]

Yousef Daneshvar, an Iranian student in Toronto, provides a Muslim affirmation for interfaith explorations:

> I could go on for hours talking about my experience of living in Toronto and being engaged in a fruitful dialogue with Christians. But let me conclude with the statement that now I believe more strongly than I did at any time before that humanity today desperately needs the help of religions to overcome the ever-growing predicaments on the globe. I can hardly imagine that religions can provide this help without conducting a serious and friendly dialogue between themselves. I think Muslims and Christians for a variety of reasons have to take more responsibility in this regard than the followers of other faiths. I know that Christians have their own scriptural and theological reasons, in addition to the practical ones, to greet the interreligious dialogue. Muslims, I believe, are stimulated to make this event happen by the Holy Qur'an. The first voice to call me to this dialogue was the Holy Qur'an that enjoined Muslims more than 1400 years ago:

Dispute not with the people of the book save
by what is the best, except for those of them
that do wrong; and say we believe in what has
been sent down to us, and what has been sent
down to you; our God and your God is one,
and to him we have surrendered. (Sura 29:46)[2]

This chapter focuses on a description of the program that
has built and continues to build interfaith bridges between
Christian and Muslim scholars such as Pierce and Daneshvar. I
will explore the span of this living dialogue in which new relationships have been built in the respective hope of two communities for a better way to relate. This dialogue of civilizations is
an attempt to create a parallel history not formed from the en-
mity based on violent images in the news media and the trail of
wars and contentions we call history. This encounter attempts
proactively to create a new kind of history together. My survey
first reviews the structure of the student exchange program, then
I reflect on the program's theological and social dimensions.

THE STRUCTURE OF THE PROGRAM

History—building a bridge of trust from both sides

The story begins with the aftermath of Iran's tragic earthquake of 1991. MCC responded to the massive humanitarian
needs created by the earthquake by distributing relief aid to
earthquake victims through co-operation with the Iranian Red
Crescent Society. MCC also sent a couple with medical training
to work under the Red Crescent's supervision with earthquake
victims for six months. This initial partnership began a series of
encounters with Iranian officials out of which emerged the vision for a student exchange. In April 1997, MCC signed an agreement with the Imam Khomeini Education and Research Institute
(IKERI) in Qom for a student exchange program to begin in 1998.
Under terms of the exchange, two North American students
would be hosted in Qom for the study of Islam and the Persian
language, while two Iranian students would be hosted for doc-
toral studies in religion in Toronto, Canada.[3]

The current structure of the bridge

MCC Area Director for Central and South Asia, Ed Martin, and Ayatollah Misbah, who heads up the IKERI, have been at the center of this programmatic bridge since its inception. These two have worked to imagine the overall structure of the program, have selected persons who would participate in it, and have continued to oversee the program. Their cordial relationship of trust forged over many years of meetings and visits has provided the stability that enables the program to continue despite many challenges.

Standing behind Ed Martin and Ayatollah Misbah on this bridge are the coordinators of the exchange in Toronto and Qom. An important aspect of the program is that the host community covers all of the housing, study, medical, and financial needs of the exchange students. While essential, this structure has provided many logistical and cross-cultural challenges for the coordinators of the program in both countries. Susan Harrison, a graduate student at the University of Toronto who has studied in the Middle East, coordinates the program on the Toronto side. Mr. Haghani, a cleric and professor of psychology in Qom who had studied in Canada, coordinates logistics in Qom. Both Harrison and Haghani repeatedly faced various forms of the skeptical question, "You're doing what?" in their efforts to set up and coordinate this program in these two locations.

The current Iranian students at the University of Toronto are Yousef Daneshvar and Mohammad Faramani. Yousef and Mohammad are pursuing doctorates in philosophy of religion while living with their families in Ontario, Canada. The North American students in the exchange have been Roy Hange and Maren Tyedmers Hange, Wallace and Evelyn Shellenberger, and Matthew and Laurie Pierce. Iranian families participating in this exchange program have been challenged by living in a very secular, Western context, in which they frequently find themselves confronted by questions of ritual uncleanliness. North American women in Qom, meanwhile, must wear the chador, and men and women alike face being considered ritually unclean by some Iranians.

Many professors have interacted with the students on both sides of the exchange. In Toronto, Professors A. James Reimer and Lydia Harder of Conrad Grebel College have worked with the two Iranian students and have put much energy into planning the conferences that have been a part of the program. In Qom, Professor Tewfiqi, a professor of Christianity, has engaged with the students since 1998, and Professor Muhammad Legenhausen has walked with the MCC students, providing invaluable insights from his unique awareness of both the Iranian Shi'ite and the Western Christian worlds.

The vision and initiative MCC expressed in sponsoring the student exchange program in Iran was profound, dramatic, and uniquely appropriate for meeting the peacemaking needs of the post-Cold War era in which religion has become the focus of much conflict. The student exchange program is designed as an ongoing encounter of the scholars who will help shape the future of each religion's view of the other. It is a proactive effort to lay the foundation for interreligious peace in two communities at once.

Mutual hosting

The exchange program has developed a structure of a living dialogue very different from the occasional dialogues I have witnessed in Qom, where Western scholars fly in for a few days and then fly out again. In this dialogue there is a daily encounter of persons of faith, not just a scholarly encounter of faith perspectives at occasional academic conferences. There is a need and a valid place, to be sure, for these academic encounters, but there is a greater need for the living dialogue in which stories about each other are read in relationships and enter the peer review and memory of the respective communities. *rather than Scholarly encounter*

Participants in the exchange each become part of the other community through mutual hosting. All of the housing, food, and monetary needs are met by their host community. The program is designed as a creative community of scholars in an effort to lay the foundations for interreligious peace by combining elements of ongoing interfaith, international, and inter-cultural dialogue in a way that becomes part of the structured life of the other community. The exchange program develops a structure within the other religious community that becomes the context for a living dialogue. Participants in this program become part of a community of shared awareness with connections in both communities.

Deepening encounter through conferences

To deepen the impact of the exchange, conferences have been held between Iranian and Mennonite scholars. The first was hosted by the Toronto Mennonite Theological Centre at the University of Toronto in October 2002 on the theme of "The Challenges of Modernity." The second was hosted by IKERI in Qom in February 2004 on the theme of "Revelation and Authority."[4]

As both traditions have wrestled with the impact of modernity on revelation and authority in their own communities, the way different aspects of the struggle played out helped the participants learn more about themselves and the other community.

Visits made during the conferences unintentionally illustrated the themes. In 2002, the Iranian scholars were taken to visit a conservative Mennonite family farm whose dress, work, and family practices rejected aspects of modernity for reasons of faith and contrasted significantly with Toronto, one of the most modern, secular, and cosmopolitan cities in the world. Later the Iranian scholars were taken to a Mennonite church for a Sunday morning service where they were warmly welcomed, yet where some of the youth were wearing clothing that was distinctly modern and immodest from an Iranian Muslim's perspective.

In 2004, the Mennonite scholars were taken as guests of honor to the grandstands for the celebration of the twenty-fifth anniversary of the Islamic revolution in Iran and were seated between the military attachés from the countries who sell weapons to Iran and the clerics who run the country by joining revelation and political authority. The Mennonite scholars also met persons who thought religion and politics should be kept separate in Iran for the sake of preserving the dignity of Islam. Both sides at the conferences saw the living paradoxes in the other's context that reflected the conference themes.[5]

Claiming deep hope for transformation

One of the intangible components of the exchange has been the mutual development of a certain finesse in intercultural, interfaith diplomacy. This happens through the kind of encounter that both acknowledges the perspective of the other and the evident differences in a way that does not offend but further illumines both parties. This often involves intentional work at sav-

ing face and building trust. The critical role of continually showing honor, respect, and consideration helps move the encounter
forward through awkward and difficult subjects. These efforts
show a basic consideration that honors the dignity of the other in
ways that daily prove there is a mutual benefit in the encounter.
Relating in such a way can create a community in consideration
even of deep differences. Such an encounter reflects the deep
hope of a better understanding between the two faith traditions.

Speaking to the Other

In both Iran and North America, participants in the exchange have had the opportunity to speak before audiences
from the other faith. Yousef Daneshvar has found the time to
speak at numerous Mennonite and other church settings. He has
communicated well and diplomatically, honoring differences
while speaking as a Muslim about the realities and dilemmas he
sees in our world.

During their time in Qom, Wally and Evie Shellenberger
were able to speak in many settings. Once, at a university hall before a few hundred students, they were asked a question about
the meaning of turning the other cheek in Jesus' teachings. They
responded by acting out Walter Wink's interpretation of this
passage that shows how Jesus' injunction preserves the dignity
of the person being hit and demands a relationship of equal status. After the Iranian clerics finished translating each step in the
drama and gave the final synopsis, the students gave them a
standing ovation to honor the way they helped bring alive the
teachings of Jesus, whom they honor as a prophet.

THEOLOGICAL REFLECTIONS

Is there a parallel between the form of the exchange and the
formation of Abrahamic leaders? Understanding the thick dialogue that is a part of this exchange is aided by reflecting on this
encounter as similar to the life formation of the leaders in Judaism, Christianity, and Islam. Here we will see that monothe-
ism is not always aided by mono-cultural formation and experiences.

Is there a blessing in the dislocation that comes with such encounters? In my experience over the years with the participants

in this exchange, I have heard many testimonies to ways participants have been challenged and blessed by the encounter.

Maybe one way to understand the blessing in this exchange
is by noting the resonance with elements of the formation of the
leaders of the Abrahamic traditions. All three Abrahamic leaders—Moses, Jesus and Muhammad—were formed amid religious difference and learned to be comfortable in multiple
worlds. Their identity and enculturation were opened by life experiences not encapsulated in one family, one culture, or one nation, creating a uniquely generative awareness of the Other.

Removed from his Hebrew family as an infant, Moses was
raised by a member of Pharaoh's family in the Egyptian royal
court, then lived in a desert tribe in the Sinai. He later returned to
offer his people a way out of their bondage based in part on his
abilities to move with understanding between worlds.

Jesus grew up with the stigma of being conceived out of
wedlock. He spent his first three years in another country, Egypt,
was raised in the "Galilee of the Gentiles," and in the first act of
his ministry was almost thrown off of a cliff for saying that God
had sent prophets to other than Jesus' own people.

Muhammad, for his part, was orphaned and raised by an
uncle. He spent many of his early working years traveling on
trading routes between the Hijaz and Damascus, where he had
regular contact with Jews and Christians, especially the monk
Bahira in the monastery at Basra in southern Syria.

The self-understanding and sense of God of these leaders
was shaped by encounter with those from different backgrounds. Each leader either was hosted by religious communities not his own or advocated for a more moderate position than
the norm. A weakness implied by these observations is that most
of the religious seminaries of these three traditions today provide little context for relating to religious difference as a part of
the formation of their respective clerics. Participants in this exchange often find themselves advocating for a more moderate
position in relation to the religious other than their own communities feel comfortable with.

Strengthening faith identity

Encounter with Muslims has strengthened the Christian
identity and conviction of the Mennonites involved. This is

partly because of the distance between Christians and Muslims. That is, when Christians talk with Christians of other traditions, they assume the beliefs and traditions they hold in common and discuss the ten percent or so that may be different.

Yet in encounter between Muslims and Christians, the common ground of belief may be only ten percent. The discussion of the broader range of differences strengthens faith awareness on both sides of the encounter, because it sharpens the understanding of one's own faith as it clarifies distinctions with the other faith. This dynamic follows the pattern of the formation of most Scripture, which can be seen as a dialogical witness when read in its original context. Thus, for example, the Genesis creation story is a polemical transformation of the Babylonian creation myth.

Goals and themes of the program

As interfaith contact is one of the least deliberately developed contact zones in the world at the local and international level (compared to interaction in the fields of business, diplomacy, culture/arts, sports, and education), the peacemaking goal of the program was to deepen the contact zone between Iranian Muslims and North American Christians. Elements of this encounter have included learning how to agree to disagree; moving beyond reaction to learning from each other; building a common perspective beyond respective religious identities; exchanging religious "ambassadors" for the sake of living dialogue; working the angles of trust; learning to see beyond our frames; and speaking and listening in the setting of the Other. This all has been done with the conviction that religious peacemakers in each faith have to do more of the work of peacemaking, since politicians and diplomats often do not or cannot speak the language of the faith communities.

Honoring the witness of the other

I have also been impressed by the kindness, hospitality, and faith of the Iranian people. I have met many Muslims who were striving as best they could to be faithful to what they understood to be the way of God. As a Christian I disagreed with many elements of that faith, but I could not help but honor the faithfulness I saw in our friends and our colleagues: the desire to honor and worship God as they knew God.

The continuum in both communities

Participants in the exchange have learned about the continuum of perspectives in both communities, a continuum that stretches from those who eagerly engage the religious outsiders to those who were deeply suspicious and thought the exchange did not merit the time or effort. Some in both the Mennonite and Iranian Shi'ite communities wanted to talk to each other despite our differences; others in the two traditions did not want to engage the other. I found that among those who sought out engagement, a new community of concern for peace and our common humanity emerged.

The question of freedom

Muslim friends repeatedly ask, "What is this freedom that the West wants to promote, this freedom that has left so much moral and social chaos in most countries in the West?" Is true freedom, as our Muslim friends argued, the freedom given in our relationships by religious and moral dictates? Or is freedom the openness and opportunity to have an owned faith so that restraint comes from inward conviction, not outward compulsion? We often sensed in these conversations the tension between the individual and corporate sense of social norms.

The evangelism/dawa question

The question of evangelism on the part of Christians and *dawa*, or invitation, on the part of Muslims has come up a number of times during this program. I remember a conversation in a seminar context in which a Muslim participant said, "We will honor and take you more seriously in this encounter if we know that you are so convinced of your faith that you would want us to become Christian, and we would invite you to understand that we take our faith so close to our hearts that we would like you to become Muslim." That sentence opened the way to a long and fascinating discussion about the role of conviction in interfaith encounter.

Elisha and border-crossing prophetic challenges

At times the trust forged by the exchange has enabled quite frank exchanges about the threat of militant Islam on the part of the North Americans and the threat of Western military power on the part of the Iranians. Just as the relationship built when Elisha healed Naaman the Syrian general enabled Elisha to enter the Syrian royal court in Damascus and challenge the violence of King Ben-Hadad (2 Kings 8: 7ff), so the relationships built in this exchange have enabled frank encounter about the violence we do to each other at the political level. Once, over a meal at a friend's home, an Iranian guest discussed how his brother had been killed in a military exchange helped by an attack from the West. The tears and words in that exchange were as vivid as Elisha's in verse 12 of the above passage, in which the sense of "how could you" is expressed corporately.

CONCLUSION

The encounter between North American Mennonites and Iranian Shi'ites is now over a decade old and, with God's grace, will continue for many more years. As the program continues to evolve, there will be practical, theological, and social matters to consider.

Practically, the exchange has moved beyond the functionality of regular visiting student programs to creating intentional communities of ongoing interfaith discussion.

Theologically, just as the prophet Jonah was challenged to see the tears of repentance of the Assyrians he did not consider worthy of God's grace, and just as readers of the book of Revelation are challenged to see that even those who pierced Jesus with a sword will see him and grieve (Rev. 1:7), so Scripture always challenges us to look beyond our narrow expectations of who can know repentance and who can see God

Socially, as North American families and institutions have encountered Iranian families and institutions, an appreciation for our shared humanity has emerged. We have developed a greater sense of the inevitable tensions arising from different conceptions of political goods—be it the Mennonite tendency to hold up freedom and democracy or the Iranian Shi'ite tendency to stress the need for a faith-ordered society and socially recognized and supported moral norms.The lived encounter between Mennonites and Iranian Shi'ites fostered by this MCC-IKERI program has provided a space to live amid the tensions to which differing politico-theological perspectives give birth. The dialogue of daily life has given us hope, has given us the ability to see the good intentions of the other side. Our defensiveness stilled, we can then live with more ambiguity and laughter alongside each other, rather than construing all differences as clashes.

I have seen the hope and vision of this exchange grow significantly from tentative trust and sometimes tense encounter when I was a part of this program's beginning in 1998 to the laughter-filled encounters that were part of the conference in Qom in February 2004. I look forward to seeing how this hope, vision, and structure will deepen and be replicated in other relational frontiers in our world.

NOTES

1. Matthew Pierce, "Dialogue Means Friendship," *MCC Peace Office Newsletter* 36/1 (Jan.-March 2006): 5.

2. Yousef Daneshvar, "An Intellectual Journey," *MCC Peace Office Newsletter* 31/3 (July-Sept. 2001): 12.

3. A more detailed account of the development and structure of this program can be found in Ed Martin's articles, "Building Bridges: the Shia of Iran and the Mennonites of North America," *MCC Peace Office Newsletter* 36/1 (Jan.-March 2006): 1-2 and "MCC and Iran," *MCC Peace Office Newsletter* 31/3 (July-September 2001): 1-3.

4. See the *Toronto Mennonite Theological Centre Newsletter* 11/1 (Summer 2003) and *Toronto Mennonite Theological Centre Newsletter* 12/1 (Oct. 2004) and *The Conrad Grebel Review* 2/3 (Fall 2003).

5. A follow-up conference in Waterloo, Ontario, hosted by MCC, received widespread coverage in the Canadian press after Iranians in Canada disrupted public meetings at the conference, protesting MCC's involvement with IKERI and denouncing the Iranian regime. In 2006 and 2007, MCC also engaged in other high-profile events concerning Iran, including hosting a meeting in New York with Iranian President Mahmoud Ahmadinejad and helping organize an ecumenical delegation to Iran in February 2007.

Chapter 8

An Ingrafting: Mennonite Central Committee and the Churches of Egypt and Syria

Eldon Wagler and Jane Emile-Wagler

MCC is an intravenous injection—not coming to plant and transplant. MCC gives us strength from the inside.
—Bishop Thomas, Coptic [Egyptian] Orthodox Church

There is a great deal of unity in the church. It's a unity, not on an organizational level, but on a spiritual level, a unity of people like us [Syrian Orthodox and Mennonites] who have Christ in our hearts.
—Patriarch Ignatius Zakka I, Syrian Orthodox Church

For decades, Mennonite Central Committee has carried out educational, community development, and peace programs in partnership with indigenous churches in the predominately Muslim countries of Egypt and Syria. In Egypt, MCC works through the programs and institutions of the Coptic Orthodox and Coptic Evangelical Churches. In Syria, MCC is sponsored by the Syrian

Orthodox Church and operates under its auspices. In neither country does MCC have programs that it directly owns. In the words of Bishop Thomas of the Coptic Orthodox Church, MCC works not "to plant and transplant" but to strengthen churches "from the inside." Or, to turn Bishop Thomas' agronomic metaphor slightly, MCC strives for an ingrafting of MCC's work into the witness of the Middle East's churches, as a celebration of the spiritual unity Patriarch Zakka has identified among us, a spiritual unity we are called to celebrate when it appears and to work for when it is absent.

An emphasis on strengthening indigenous churches from the inside is typical of MCC work around the world, not just in the Middle East generally or Syria and Egypt specifically. In many countries where MCC operates, the local churches with which MCC works are products of Mennonite mission efforts. In Syria and Egypt, however, MCC primarily partners with branches of Orthodoxy, a family of Christianity with which Mennonites traditionally have had little contact geographically, historically, or emotionally. Mennonites and Orthodox seem outwardly to be at opposite ends of the ecclesiological spectrum. This chapter explores how and why MCC has negotiated these differences, while also discussing the implications of these ecumenical partnerships for interfaith matters, specifically Christian-Muslim interactions.

MCC'S FIRST ENCOUNTERS IN EGYPT

MCC made its first foray into the religiously and ethnically diverse Middle Eastern/Mediterranean thicket in the middle of the twentieth century, drawn by the refugee crises of World War II. The first MCC program in Egypt began in 1943, with fifteen volunteers working with European refugees in the Suez Canal Zone. MCC personnel left Egypt in 1954. In these early stages of MCC involvement in Egypt, workers had minimal contact with Egyptians. Most of MCC's initial participation was in cooperation with international and government agencies, not with Egyptian churches.

The story of MCC interaction with the Eastern churches only begins later, in Crete. Greece is not usually considered part of the Middle East, but it is certainly part of the Orthodox world. It was in Crete, Greece's largest island, that MCC workers first cut their teeth on significant cooperation and partnership with Orthodox churches. Beginning in 1965, MCC embarked on a partnership with the Greek Orthodox Church in Crete on agricultural projects. MCC remained active in Crete until 1977, when it withdrew all personnel and turned the agricultural ventures over to community organizations.

Robert Kreider and Rachel Waltner Goossen called the MCC involvement in Crete "one of the most unusual programs in MCC's history."[1] The program was extraordinary at the time because it worked entirely through institutions of the Greek Orthodox Church and because MCC turned the program over completely to Greeks after a little more than decade of involvement. "MCC came to Crete at the invitation of the bishop to help for a limited time in an agricultural development program and left Crete after reaching its minimal objectives. MCC's contribution may be measured less in agricultural productivity than in the warm relationships between volunteers and the orthodox people of Crete."[2]

Meanwhile, MCC had its first serious engagement with Egyptian Christians in 1969, when Harry Martens, MCC Middle East Commissioner, met with government and church officials to discuss the issues arising from the flood of refugees following the 1967 war with Israel. Martens met Egyptian church leaders representing both the Orthodox and the Protestant communions, including most significantly Coptic Pope Kyrollos VI and Bishop Samuel, who were in charge of ecumenical relations and social services for the Coptic Orthodox Church. Bishop Samuel also headed the Ecumenical Advisory Council for Church Services (EACCS).[3]

Martens recommended that MCC funds and material aid to refugees be directed to EACCS, with only biannual visits from MCC representatives. Martens' recommendation was significant in that he believed the relief work could be carried out entirely through local administration. While perhaps tinged with naïveté, Martens' vision was a commendable shift from the colonialist mindset that all administration of projects had to be done by expatriate personnel, and it was roughly in line with what was taking place across the Mediterranean Sea on the island of Crete. Martens' vision also included the suggestion that two delegates from the Coptic Orthodox Church be invited to visit and speak with North American MCC constituents. A full ten years later in 1979, Bishop Samuel finally made the trek to the United States as a guest of MCC.[4]

While the MCC-Coptic Orthodox relationship was on a slow track in the 1970s, there was another generally parallel track developing with the Presbyterian Church of Egypt. Urbane Peachey was the MCC Country Representative in Amman who administered program in Jordan. Peachey traveled to Egypt in 1970 and arranged for the placement of MCC teachers with a Presbyterian school in Cairo. In 1973, four MCC teachers arrived in Cairo in the early fall, just before the outbreak of the October 1973 war. MCC volunteer workers in Egypt were supervised from Amman until the arrival of Gerald Brunk in 1975 as Country Representative.[5]

Toward the end of the 1970s, Bishop Samuel established an English as a Foreign Language (EFL) program at the Coptic Orthodox cathedral in Cairo. In 1979 Bishop Samuel requested MCC's assistance in organizing and teaching at the fledgling EFL institute. MCC teacher John Derksen, the first MCCer seconded to a Coptic Orthodox institution, arrived to help organize the cathedral's EFL program. In addition to his work in Cairo, Derksen also traveled regularly to St. Makarios' Monastery in Wadi Natrun in the early 1980s. There he taught English classes to monks residing in this desert monastery.

Remarkably, more than half of the eighty monks at St. Makarios also signed up for Derksen's class on Reformation History. When Bishop Samuel was slain in October 1981 in the same hail of bullets that killed President Anwar Sadat, MCC Middle East Secretary Urbane Peachey fondly recalled Bishop Samuel as "our bishop."[6]

By the late 1980s, the Coptic Orthodox-MCC partnership had evolved to the point that placements at Coptic Orthodox institutions were roughly equal to those at various Protestant organizations. Vern Ratzlaff, who served as MCC Country Representative in Egypt from 1982 to 1987, is recalled fondly among Coptic Orthodox leaders for his remarkable love of Egypt and sympathetic understanding of the Coptic Orthodox Church. Upon completion of his term in country and his return to Canada, Ratzlaff penned a set of reflections introducing the Coptic Orthodox Church to Mennonites. "In Egypt," Ratzlaff wrote, "Mennonites have—in language, at least—tended to model servanthood rather than partnership. MCC does not have its own programs but limits itself to working through existing church institutions. . . . assisting the local church in carrying out its self-perceived mandate and agenda."[7]

MCC'S FIRST CONTACTS IN SYRIA

Ed Epp, an MCC administrator stationed in Amman, Jordan, began making the trip up to Syria to visit church leaders in Damascus in the late 1980s. LeRoy Friesen too followed on the road to Damascus in the summer of 1988 as part of a research assignment commissioned by the Mennonite Middle East Reference Group (MMERG), a consultative body consisting of MCC and various Mennonite mission agencies.[8] Friesen visited the heads of the Syrian Orthodox, Greek Orthodox, Greek Catholic, and Armenian Orthodox in Damascus. Following his visit to Syria, Friesen strongly encouraged Mennonites to work in conjunction with and in support of Syrian churches. Given the blossoming relationships with Coptic Christians in Egypt, MCC had the requisite momentum to act on Friesen's counsel and attempt a similar arrangement for involvement in Syria. But would MCC find a church partner willing to engage MCC?

The Syrian Arab Republic was a Soviet satellite state in the 1980s, well off the beaten track for Western tourists and positioned on the fringes of Western consciousness. Syria's designation as an "enemy state" due to being in the Soviet orbit of influence was, however, something of an incentive for MCC to seek involvement in Syria, given the Mennonite understanding that Christians are to reach out to perceived enemies in love. But the prevailing political climate of the 1980s did little to encourage Syrians to seek out interaction with a Western church organization such as MCC. Syrian authorities perceived any connection to the West as suspicious; a partnership with a foreign organization was bound to raise a host of unwelcome questions for a Syrian institution.

An additional wrinkle on the Syrian landscape was the almost complete lack of a civil society outside of mosque and church. With a socialist government theoretically seeing to all the needs of its citizenry, little space was left for civil society institutions and non-governmental organizations (NGOs). A Western NGO like MCC could not register in Syria. So while MCC had a growing missiological orientation to work with and through local churches, partnership with the Syrian church was also a logistical necessity if MCC was to work in Syria. Without a Syrian church or organization being willing to support MCC and procure residency visas and permits for its workers, having a program with personnel in country would have been difficult if not impossible.

In 1990, MCC Area Secretary Ed Martin approached the Syrian Orthodox Patriarch Zakka I about a possible MCC worker placement with the church. Patriarch Zakka responded favorably and suggested that MCC place an English language instructor at St. Ephrem's Clerical Seminary. In 1991 Roy Hange moved to the seminary in Damascus as the first MCC service worker in Syria. Hange was in effect seconded to the Syrian Orthodox Church, an arrangement that still holds for MCC personnel to this day. The Syrian Orthodox Church continues to secure residency for MCC personnel, no small gesture of trust in a country where Western NGOs are still viewed with significant suspicion.

The Syrian Orthodox Church is a sister church to the Coptic Orthodox Church of Egypt—both belong to the Oriental Orthodox or non-Chalcedonian family of churches. Like MCC Egypt, having personnel work within the structures of an apostolic church has remained the *modus operandi* of MCC involvement in Syria. MCC to this day maintains no structure or institutions of its own; rather, projects are done through Syrian church institutions. This missiological stance is a response to LeRoy Friesen's call for "revolutionary subordination"[9] to Christian brothers and sisters in Syria, in the hope that MCC's gifts can be grafted into the church's witness to the Anointed One.

A PAUSE FOR MISSIOLOGICAL REFLECTION

At the same time in the late 1980s that Ratzlaff was reflecting on the Mennonite experience with the Coptic Orthodox in Egypt, LeRoy Friesen, as noted above, had been commissioned by the three main Mennonite organizations then involved in the

Middle East to do a major study of their work. This grouping of Mennonite agencies—MCC, Mennonite Board of Missions, and Eastern Mennonite Board of Missions and Charities—was the one that became known as MMERG. Friesen's study is more than a description of Mennonite involvement in the Middle East; it is also a theological reflection on the meaning of Anabaptists' faith identity when encountering other faiths and confessions.

Friesen noted that Mennonites "came to the Levant ill-prepared, either missionally or missiologicially, for the region's unparalleled ecumenical complexities and opportunities." Mennonites were accustomed, argued Friesen, to thinking of themselves as an alternative community with an "over/against" sense of the world, and often as an alternative vis-à-vis other Christians as well.[10] The early Anabaptists' experiences with persecution at the hands of fellow Christians did little to predispose twentieth-century Mennonites toward working with other denominations and naturally fed this over/against view of others, a view only exacerbated when the other denominations were "high church."

Yet despite all these historical inhibitions toward working with people from other church traditions, Friesen noted that some Mennonite agencies had begun to do so in the decades leading up to the 1990s. Friesen in particular cited the MCC Egypt program in its work with Coptic Orthodox and Coptic Evangelicals "as a profoundly ecumenical experience, one fueled by a vision for which it is not easy to account."[11] At a bare minimum, the vision for MCC work in Egypt showed a commitment to shared diaconal service and witness. It demonstrated a singular disinterest in building up a Mennonite empire, given that there were existing Egyptian Christian communities. Later in this chapter we will attempt to flesh out the impetus for ecumenical work, for the ingrafting of Mennonite witness into the ongoing witness of established local churches.

In Friesen's concluding report, he called for a strengthening of Mennonite commitment to work deliberately with Middle Eastern churches toward the "goal of together becoming increasingly conformed to the image of Jesus Christ."[12] Friesen's call was not for a cuddly ecumenism that denies all differences in an effort merely to get along. The appeal was not to be less Anabaptist and somehow more Orthodox or Catholic. This instead was the question: How could "a contemporary Mennonite be both Anabaptist in vision and also ecumenical in practice?"[13]

IMPETUS FOR INGRAFTING

Friesen pointed out that Mennonites came to the Middle East with a limited background to prepare them for interaction with others, including Christians. Indeed, among the brothers and sisters of their own Christian faith there was much to set Mennonite newcomers to the Middle East back on their heels. Aside from the obvious differences in language, society, and culture, numerous other elements were at best unfamiliar and at worst theologically disturbing to Anabaptists. Most Middle Eastern Christians belong to the Orthodox families and are liturgical in worship and hierarchical in polity. All Orthodox Christians practice infant baptism, and some still long for the Constantinian era. Communion at the Eucharistic table is closed to Mennonites. For the heirs of the Radical Reformation, there was much in the Middle Eastern Christian milieu to which they could take umbrage and which made those churches sometimes seem concerned only with supposedly "dead" ritual.

At the same time, the history of interaction between Eastern and Western Christians provides ample reasons for Middle Eastern Christians to be suspicious of Western Christians. Foremost on the list is the memory of the Crusades, in which cross-clad Christians from Western Europe descended violently on the area and forever changed the relationships between confessions. Not only were Eastern Christians killed by the invading crusaders, but the Muslims of the Middle East gradually began to associate the atrocities of the crusaders with Christianity in general. Later Christian missionaries colluded with colonialist enterprises of the eighteenth, nineteenth, and twentieth centuries. These missionaries who came ostensibly to evangelize non-Christians found it much easier to "steal sheep" from existing Christian churches, often leading to a deep distrust on the part of the Orthodox.

Despite the obvious differences between North American Anabaptists and Christians of the Middle East and the Mediterranean, Mennonite agencies decided it was preferable not to establish Mennonite congregations in the region. Rather, Mennonites decided that the missiologically sound path was to accompany the churches of the Middle East in their witness.

Two basic approaches have proved useful in bridging the divide between East and West, between Middle Eastern Christians and Mennonites: The first approach is accompanying the Middle Eastern churches through volunteer placements of MCC workers under the supervision of Syrian and Egyptian church and church-related institutions. The second approach is supporting Egyptian and Syrian initiatives with MCC resources, including material aid, financial grants, and training opportunities, such as at the Summer Peacebuilding Institute at Eastern Mennonite University.

Collaboration in diaconal ministries has formed and fostered bonds of friendship and bridges of trust between Mennonites on the one hand and Syrian and Coptic churches on the other. Engaging in common service, we should stress, does not mean pretending differences do not exist. Instead, it makes a practical declaration that a unity of service and witness precedes a need for doctrinal and organizational unity.[14] That Copts and Mennonites, and that Syrian Orthodox and Mennonites, can work together within the structures of the respective Orthodox churches is a powerful demonstration to the world that the church is indeed universal.

Service is transformative, a form of healing for past wounds that goes straight to the heart of the gospel. MCC workers and local Christians find a unity in service that far exceeds our doctrinal unity. Patriarch Zakka I, head of the Syrian Orthodox Church, noted in a January 2004 meeting with MCC workers that while we may not "come close in our theological discussions, what really matters is the contact we have, the personal relationships. This is what I believe."

This is not to say that Mennonites and Orthodox should be satisfied with the level of fellowship in conversation and in service—the current ecumenical altitude falls far short of what we are called to in Jesus' prayer for unity, "that they may all be one" (John 17:21). It is the will of Christ that Christians be one. As Christians we are to act in a manner that fosters unity of Christ's body. This is not merely the desire of people who champion unity, or the agenda of an ecumenical church council. It is the longing of Christ himself. As people who strive to take seriously

Christ's life and prayer for our ecclesial life, we cannot simply applaud ourselves because Christians from East and West serve together. The mission of the church must include working toward a greater unity, with faith in God's timing through the work of the Holy Spirit.

Another impetus for (also effectively a result of) ingrafting has been the need to discover common roots. Working together as Easterners and Westerners has been a way of discovery, or rediscovery if you will, of the common stuff from which we are all formed. Anabaptists need little fine-tuning to receive stories of martyrdom. Suffering has been wired into the Mennonite narrative and helps make Mennonites receptive to stories of Copts and Syrians enduring persecution, many of them far fresher than the *Martyrs' Mirror* accounts Mennonites bear. In addition, we encounter the similarities in our stories which have at times been hidden by a particular telling of history.[15] Anabaptists, for instance, sometimes chart church history as a relative lull between the first Christians and the sixteenth-century Reformation in Europe. In the haste to get to the Reformation, the Anabaptist story loses the richness of the patristic ages. Conversation with Orthodox Christians who drink deeply from these wells of spirituality is a dialogue that enhances Anabaptist sensibilities of God at work in all of church history.

COMPLICATIONS OF INGRAFTING

MCC's decision to work in Egypt and Syria through local churches has been a road marked by mutually expanding horizons and by life-changing encounters. This is not to imply that mutual understanding has been faultless. In 2005, an Orthodox bishop told a visiting journalist in Syria: "I don't really know what to say when people ask me who the Mennonites are except that they love God and God loves them." Because there are no Mennonite churches in the Middle East, and given that MCC works through local structures in Egypt and Syria, significant identity issues can arise with partners and with the society in general.

Mennonites themselves at times have wished "for the tangible benefits involving identity and continuity that an institutional presence can provide. That we Mennonites tended to travel light rendered our ministry more rich and versatile, but it also left us vulnerable to self-doubts as to our purpose in the region."[16] At times we as Mennonites have not been sufficiently clear about our identities and the purpose of our presence in the Middle East. Little wonder, then, that our Syrian and Egyptian partners are not always clear about who we are.

Furthermore, an asymmetry often colors relationships between MCCers and the Orthodox. Anabaptists typically cluster at the bottom of hierarchical ecclesiastical structures. The Orthodox churches are deeply hierarchical, with structures that have settled into place over many long centuries. As Mennonites have tried to in-graft their work into Orthodox structures, it has meant dealing with men of the cloth whose roles carry extraordinary weight and who wield significant power in their communities. The formalities extended to Orthodox clergymen have certainly expanded MCCers' horizons, but then for patriarchs and bishops to sit in discussion at the table with Mennonite laymen and women has undoubtedly stretched the clergymen as well, given that they typically deal with church and government dignitaries in more formal settings.

Asymmetry exists in other areas as well. Despite MCC's best intentions to become enmeshed appropriately and sensitively in Syrian and Egyptian church structures, the fact remains that MCC is a Western NGO with money and resources. MCC workers can face the temptation of a quick fix by throwing money at a situation, an intervention that can sap the vitality of local initiative. Vern Ratzlaff astutely points out that access to money and people "means power. The availability of such resources may well corrupt both partners, not in a moral sense but in a subversive sense."[17]

A final potential problem facing MCC's stance of working inside and through Middle Eastern churches is that it may cause those same churches to be seen by the local society as siding with the West and becoming a "fifth column" for outsiders. An unintentional effect of MCC's work could be the further marginalization of churches that already have their nationalist loyalties questioned by their Muslim compatriots.[18]

INTERFAITH IMPLICATIONS OF INGRAFTING

The history of the West's interface in the Middle East has too often been one of aggression and opportunism. Sadly, the Western church has been party to this, with the Crusades serving as the most egregious example. Muslims certainly began thinking differently of their indigenous Christian neighbors after waves of Western Christian crusaders descended on them. The legacy of the Crusades is writ large on the consciousness of the people of the Middle East, where the grievances of centuries past possess an immediacy difficult for Western amnesiacs to imagine.

Mennonites can make a significant statement to Muslims by being servants to the Middle Eastern churches and by not exercising the conventional power practices of the West. Doing so, suggests Ratzlaff, draws "the attention of the Muslim population to the local church and not to the strength of an independent Western movement whose independence is commentary on the irrelevance of the local church and thus marginalizes Egyptian leaders, institutions, and people."[19] MCC's choice to accompany the Syrian and Coptic churches is not without possible drawbacks in Muslim eyes, as noted above. Ideally, by accompanying the churches of the Middle East, MCC contributes to the vitality of the church in its varied contexts. A vital, dynamic church can in turn engage its Muslims neighbors and compatriots in a spirit of openness, confidence, and non-defensiveness.

One of MCC's goals through its ingrafting into Syrian and Egyptian churches has been to support continued local Christian presence in the Middle East. At their own peril, Western Christians sometimes forget that Christianity sprang from the Middle East, then spread to the West: The original Bethlehem, after all, is not in Pennsylvania! Muslim Middle Easterners often fall into the same trap of understanding Christianity as a Western institution. The presence of vital indigenous Christian churches serves as a concrete corrective to the Muslim tendency to dismiss Christianity as an essentially Western reality. Predominately Islamic societies need the Christian Other in their midst because, as Riad Jarjour, former General Secretary of the Middle East Council of Churches noted, "it is difficult for each person to keep a balanced view of the other's religion."[20]

Saudi Arabian Prince Talal bin Abdul Aziz al-Saud, meanwhile, is one Muslim who argues eloquently that Muslims need

Christians living among them. He decries the hemorrhage of Middle Eastern Christians from the region as a loss of meaningful and necessary diversity, observing that "the emigration of Arab Christians, if it continues, is a profound blow against the very heart of our future. It is our urgent task to bring this emigration to a halt."[21]

Finally, not only Muslims stand to gain from having Christians living in their midst. Western Christians as well can benefit from Egyptian and Syrian Christians' long experience of living in the house of Islam. For Christians in the United States, the need for serious engagement with Islam has been greatly heightened by the events of September 11, 2001. To engage with Islam not only religiously, but also politically, socially, and culturally—in a way that avoids the colonialist approaches of the past—is a new frontier for most Westerners.

The Christians generally best qualified to speak to questions raised by engagements with Muslims are those with the most significant firsthand experience of the matter—Christians of the Middle East. An Orthodox bishop in Damascus told MCC workers in 2005, "You in the West are good at reading about Muslims. You discuss Islam. But we here live with Muslims. We might not read much about them, but we have a living discussion with them." Our hope is that the presence of Mennonites working alongside and in-grafted into Syrian and Egyptian churches that are living out interreligious commitments will help build bridges of understanding between Muslims and Christians.

MENNONITE COPTIC COMMITTEE?

A cassette tape vendor in Cairo once mentioned in casual conversation that he knew an American English teacher named Kent Beck. The tape seller went on to say that he thought Kent was a really good man, and that he worked for an organization called Mennonite Coptic Committee! MCC undoubtedly means different things to different people, and the Muslim tape vendor's remark raises an important issue: Just how mutual is MCC prepared to be in its international programs? How Coptic can MCC be? Or how Syrian Orthodox? How Mennonite should MCC be? What is a healthy balance between a strong connection to the sending agency and a vigorous receptivity to the local landscape? What models are there for being accountable to both?

MCC in Egypt and Syria endeavors to have it both ways by ingrafting through service into Coptic and Syrian Orthodox churches. The healthy tension that arises from joining two diverse religious traditions is something MCC workers and partners live daily. This mingling in common diaconal service is holy, fertile ground for growth in Christ, our true vine.

NOTES

1. Robert S. Kreider and Rachel Waltner Goossen, *Hungry, Thirsty and a Stranger* (Scottdale, Pa.: Herald Press, 1988), 213.

2. Ibid., 222.

3. Linda Herr, "Connecting Anabaptists and Copts: The MCC-Coptic Orthodox Church Relationship," *MCC Peace Office Newsletter* 36/2 (April-June 2006): 2-4.

4. Karen Cressman Anderson, "Chronological History of MCC Egypt," unpublished (June 2003), 1. Available at the MCC Egypt office in Cairo.

5. Ibid., 1-2.

6. Herr, "Connecting Anabaptists and Copts."

7. Vern Ratzlaff, *The Coptic Orthodox Church: Five Essays*, MCC Occasional Paper No. 1 (May 1988), 26.

8. Friesen's research eventually resulted in his study, *Mennonite Witness in the Middle East: A Missiological Introduction*, 2nd. ed. (Elkhart, Ind.: Mennonite Mission Network, 2000, 2nd. edition).

9. Friesen, *Mennonite Witness in the Middle East*, 172.

10. Ibid., 173.

11. Ibid., 176

12. Ibid., 179.

13. Ibid., 174.

14. Mennonite Central Committee itself is a testimony to the fact that diverse groups of Mennonites, Amish, and Brethren in Christ can collaborate in serving others, despite rather obvious differences in practice and polity.

15. Gideon Goosen. *Bringing Churches Together: A Popular Introduction to Ecumenism*, 2nd. ed. (Geneva: WCC Publications, 2001), 8.

16. Friesen, *Mennonite Witness in the Middle East*, 84-85.

17. Ratzlaff, *The Coptic Orthodox Church*, 9.

18. Jonathan Kuttab quoted in "Arab Christians Are Nationalists, Not 'Fifth Columnists,'" *The Daily Star* (Nov. 28, 2005).

19. Ratzlaff, *The Coptic Orthodox Church*, 29.

20. Riad Jarjour, quoted in Betty Jane Bailey and J. Martin Bailey, "The Future of Christians in the Arab World," *Who are the Christians of the Middle East?* (Grand Rapids: Wm. B. Eerdmans, 2003), 20.

21. Prince Talal bin Abdul Aziz al-Saud, "Keeping Arab Christians Here" *MECC NewsReport* 14/1 (Summer 2002), 30; trans. Lew Scudder from Arabic, *An-Nahar* newspaper, Beirut (Jan. 29, 2002).

Chapter 9

Mennonite Experience with Interfaith and Ecumenical Work in Southeast Europe

Randall Puljek-Shank

*I*n early 1993, front lines divided the former Yugoslav republics from one another and almost all forms of communication were blocked. Church leaders who had studied, worked, and fellowshipped together found themselves divided as well. In this situation, a small but significant event took place: a meeting of Christians from all sides. This one short event, lost amid the din of competing politics and armies, was possible because of a sustained focus on developing relationships. The results of this event, like a recurring theme, can be heard today many years later as this work of connecting peoples continues.

In this essay I will discuss how Mennonite Central Committee (MCC) has supported interfaith and ecumenical bridge-building efforts in its over forty-year history of working in southeast Europe. I will give particular attention to the countries of the former Yugoslavia, especially Bosnia and Herzegovina, Croatia, and Serbia, although at times MCC regional work has included other countries (such as Albania and Hungary). I am an "insider" currently working as the co-representative for MCC in southeast Europe. I am thus not neutral with respect to the projects and events I describe. I have attempted to tell the story of MCC-supported interfaith involvements rather than presenting an academic analysis of these projects. The story I tell reflects the perspectives of some of the principal actors, whom I interviewed while preparing this essay.[1]

MCC's engagement in interfaith and intrafaith work can be divided into three distinct periods: 1948 to 1990, 1991 to 1995, and 1996 to the present. MCC first became engaged in the region of southeast Europe in Hungary in 1948, and in Yugoslavia in 1963 with relief following the Skopje earthquake. From these early beginnings onwards, MCC's work has focused on relief and economic development projects, with an emphasis on partnership with local religious, particularly Christian, groups. This work focused on the former Yugoslavia from 1990 on in response to the wars of Yugoslav Succession. Interfaith and intrafaith efforts have been a particularly significant part of this response.

In the area of the former Yugoslavia, Protestant groups like the Baptists and Pentecostals are the oldest MCC partners. More recently, MCC has forged partnerships with Bosnian Catholic Franciscans, the Serbian Orthodox Church, and the Bosnian Muslim charity, Merhamet.

However, before starting to tell the story of MCC's involvement with these bodies, one must first describe the context in which MCC commitments have unfolded. The former Yugoslavia lies on one of the historic religious fault lines, where Roman Catholicism, Orthodox Christianity, and Islam have each had significant historical and contemporary influence. These differences served as contributing factors in the brutal wars of the 1990s, collectively called the wars of Yugoslav Succession. However, depicting these conflicts as primarily religious or even as ethnic wars is, I believe, profoundly misleading. A more astute analysis must consider economic and other social dynamics (for example, the role of rapid industrialization and the division between rural and urban populations) as contributing factors for the wars of succession.

The fact remains that religious leaders, institutions, symbols, and identities were all very visible before, during, and after these wars. The prominent role of religion places a special burden on the relief, community development, and peace efforts of a church-related organization such as MCC. As Christians committed to Jesus' way of peace, Mennonite workers asked themselves how MCC work might foster strong interfaith relations.

However, interfaith cooperation and dialogue was not something Mennonites from outside came to teach. A rich tradition of interreligious tolerance was already at hand, a tradition, Misha Glenny describes, referring to the city of Sarajevo, as "one of Europe's greatest achievements . . . where East and West not only tolerated but thrived off each other's cultural influence."[2] MCC's work in the region has been one of supporting local partners in rediscovering, enabling, strengthening, and renewing these traditions of tolerance, cooperation, and neighborliness across religious and ethnic lines.

MCC, of course, is an initiative of North American Mennonites. As a North American organization working in southeast Europe, where does MCC envision the locus of interfaith bridge-building work to be? If the locus of intervention is inside of southeast Europe, is the focus on building ties between the religious communities of the region (a subset of which is ecumenical work among the region's Christian communities), or on building ties between local religious communities and Mennonite and others from North America? As we will see, both forms of bridge building have been part of MCC's work. Because MCC also carries out educational efforts among its supporting constituency in North America through speaking tours and publishing ventures, potential bridges of connection are being forged between Mennonite and Brethren in Christ churches in the United States and Canada and religious communities in southeast Europe.

HISTORICAL BACKGROUND

While MCC's deliberate interfaith work began much later, the story of MCC's engagement with interfaith matters in the region began with the appointment of Gerald Shenk by the Eastern Mennonite Board of Mission and Charities (now Eastern Mennonite Missions). Shenk was appointed in cooperation with MCC as a student of the sociology of religion in Zagreb, Croatia (1977-1978) and in Sarajevo, Bosnia and Herzegovina (1979 onward). An important component of Shenk's work was developing connections between Mennonites and the small Protestant churches of the region. This study assignment later led to a teaching position at the Evangelical Theological Faculty (ETF) in Croatia and the Baptist Theological Seminary in Serbia, for Gerald and his wife Sara Wenger-Shenk. ETF was and continues to be the largest theological training institution for Protestants in former Yugoslavia. Much of MCC's interfaith and ecumenical work in southeast Europe can be traced back to the relationships forged between MCC and Protestant leaders during these years.

1991–1995

In 1991, amid rising levels of separatist nationalism and growing ethnic fears and tensions, the former Yugoslavia moved toward its first multi-party elections. When Croatia declared independence in 1991 and Bosnia and Herzegovina followed in 1992, they faced Serb separatist movements which occupied large areas of these former Yugoslav republics. Ethnic cleansing—the forced expulsion of the "other" populations by intimidation, killing, and imprisonment of minority populations into concentration camps—led to waves of refugees fleeing to territories where Croats, Bosniaks, and Serbs were in the majority. As the "aggressor" in the eyes of Western governments, the government of "rump" Yugoslavia (the Republics of Serbia and Montenegro, after the secession of Republics Slovenia, Croatia, Bosnia and Herzegovina, and Macedonia) led by Slobodan Miloševic, faced economic sanctions.

Serbia became progressively isolated by other countries. MCC's first programmatic involvement in the former Yugoslavia after the Shenks' study and teaching involved work with the Serbian population, specifically support for Serb refugees in Belgrade. Gerald Shenk had visited a former ETF colleague living in Belgrade, Aleksandar Birviš, who had fled from his work as ETF Dean in Croatia as the fighting intensified. In Belgrade he found that the Baptist and Pentecostal churches of Belgrade had come together to cooperate in feeding and clothing the hundreds of thousands of refugees who had poured into Serbia. MCC decided to join in this ecumenical effort, an initiative that not only provided food and other basic supplies to refugees but also represented promising ecumenical cooperation between two churches that had sometimes been at odds. MCC's decision to support this initiative of Serbian Protestant churches also bridged the sharp divide between Serbia and the West. MCC's engagement in Serbia during these war years stood in sharp contrast to the involvements of many other international humanitarian organizations that were much more heavily, if not exclusively, focused on Croatia and Bosnia.

Another early initiative during the war years sought to foster ecumenical connections among a wide variety of Christian teachers and lay leaders from various sides of the conflict, supporting efforts to bridge ethnic, national, and ecumenical divides.With the joint sponsorship of MCC and the Life and Peace Institute of Uppsala, Sweden, Gerald Shenk, by this time a professor at the Eastern Mennonite Seminary, and David Steele visited a wide variety of church leaders on all sides of the front lines during the first half of 1993. Many persons with whom they visited were contacts Shenk had developed during his previous work with MCC. Shenk and Steele encountered many examples of misinformation and distorted perceptions during these visits. Former colleagues, now on opposite sides of the conflict, now suspected each other. Shenk and Steele concluded that it was vitally important for Christian leaders to come together to hear each other's stories in the hope that distrust and misperceptions might give way to renewed relationships.[3]

With MCC support, Shenk and Steele organized a roundtable to which ten mid-level Christian leaders were invited. Although Steele and Shenk had initially hoped to include people of other faiths in this workshop, they limited it to Christians at the recommendation of prospective participants who felt that the ecumenical differences would prove sufficiently challenging and complicated. Over the course of three days in the relatively neutral location of Vienna, the participants first shared their own stories of war and its aftermath. Slowly, mutual misperceptions gave way and trust began to build. Participants engaged in role-plays, stepping into the shoes of the other participants and later identifying aspects of their own ecclesial traditions that could contribute to peacemaking.

The Vienna conference was only one event with ten participants. However, it provided the basis for a much more extensive series of workshops from 1995 to 2001 led by David Steele and the Center for Strategic and International Studies on peacebuilding with mid-level religious leaders[4]. This project conducted meetings in Bosnia, Croatia, and Serbia with Orthodox, Catholic, and Muslim religious leaders. Although this project was conducted without MCC sponsorship, it built on the relationships MCC had already cultivated. Some local initiatives emerged from these workshops, including groups like the Interreligious Center in Belgrade, which became a key MCC partner in interfaith bridge building.

Even as MCC fostered ecumenical connections among Christian bodies committed to peace, during the early 1980s MCC also reached out beyond the church's walls in tentative interfaith engagements. In 1992, Immanuel Gitlin was working for MCC and teaching at ETF. When the ETF faculty relocated to Slovenia and later Zagreb due to fighting close to Osijek, Immanuel and his wife Helen also relocated. Desiring to reach beyond the Pentecostal community, Immanuel developed friendships in Zagreb's Jewish Center. With the encouragement of MCC, these connections developed into Gitlin teaching Hebrew at the Jewish Center as a supplement to his ETF responsibilities.

During this time, MCC also began shipping relief supplies to Bosnian refugees in Croatia through the Baptist organization Duhovna Stvarnost. These relief supplies were in turn delivered to the Bosnian Muslim refugee population in partnership with the Muslim charity, Merhamet, which itself later became an MCC partner in Bosnia. Beginning in 1995, MCC seconded Amy Gopp to the Christian Information Service in Zagreb. Through participation in ecumenical prayers, she met a Franciscan priest from Bosnia, Ivo Marković. Ivo later initiated the interreligious service Face to Face and the Pontanima interreligious choir, both of which have been valued MCC partners since 1996.

Interfaith Projects in Bosnia, 1996 – 2006

MCC connections forged during the break-up of the former Yugoslavia laid the groundwork for more explicit MCC involvement in interfaith bridge building as the active fighting ended in Croatia and Bosnia in 1995. Two significant factors contributed to MCC's decision to engage in more explicit interfaith work. The first factor was the religious dimensions of the war; the second was the potential of faith to serve as a source of hope and comfort in a situation of war.

As introduced earlier, beginning in 1996 and continuing to the present, one major MCC-supported interfaith initiative has been the Face to Face interreligious service. After Fra. Marković founded Face to Face, he invited MCC worker Amy Gopp to help him in this new initiative. In the interreligious choir Pontanima, also founded by Fra. Marković, people from all religious groups as well as those without a religious identity sing sacred songs from the Bosnian religious traditions (Catholic, Orthodox, Muslim, and Jewish).

From Pontanima's beginning, Fra. Marković and others in the choir have sought to make and nurture grassroots interreligious connections, in contrast to high-level bridge-building efforts aimed primarily at the heads of religious communities. Through public concerts, televised performances, and the distribution of Pontanima CDs, the Pontanima choir reaches out to regular members of faith communities. Pontanima has built public pressure on religious leaders during its decade of existence, pressure to work for coexistence and mutual respect instead of fostering divisions. Bosnia's religious leaders have gradually come to respect what Pontanima is and does.

Amy Gopp and later MCC workers describe the power of Pontanima as residing in and emerging from the strong bonds forged in the community of the choir. Its over sixty members were initially attracted to the choir by a desire to sing, but in Pontanima they also found a place of safety and community, one which helped give participants meaning and purpose. Gopp notes that Pontanima's power comes from the choir members getting to know each other as people and building relationships with one another. Choir members already shared strong Bosnian cultural and linguistic traditions, so they built on these traditional practices of hospitality and community as they interacted across religious boundaries with each other. Gopp, as an outsider to the culture, understood her own role in Pontanima as a pastoral one, to be an informal supportive presence through fellowship with the choir's members.

John Wall and Karin Kaufman Wall, MCC workers with Face to Face from 1999 to 2002, described their role as supporting Fra. Marković, both in raising funds and in translating Face to Face's and political leaders are the bonds of friendship and relationship forged through the Center's work. As an example of the inter-faith bridges the Center builds, she highlights being called by a Muslim Imam from the Sandžak area of Serbia to spend some time with him during a visit to Belgrade. Although the Interreligious Center's role is behind the scenes, it provides an important space for the religious groups in Serbia to be connected. Few public events of an interfaith nature occur without the Center's participation. Ajzenkol also notes the multiple sensitivities each group brings to interfaith encounters. Only by making sure to spend time nurturing relationships, she observes, can one know what the delicate points of contention might be.

In addition to organizing workshops in which religious leaders gather to share about their faith traditions and to explore how their faiths might be resources for peacebuilding, the Inter-religious Center has also carried out a wide variety of public out-reach. This includes publication of an interfaith calendar featuring descriptions of all of the region's religious holidays and the creation of an interactive CD with information about the religious practices, traditions, and theologies of Serbia's different faith communities.

In reflecting on her work, Ajzenkol believes that it is easier for a woman to be engaged in her role. Although the religious clergy are almost exclusively male, she is able to function effectively behind the scenes. She finds that her work requires a lot of patience; occasional weariness lives alongside ongoing enthusiasm.

MCC worker Harold Otto also worked to promote reconciliation among evangelical groups in the region. During the wars, Serbian, Croatian, and Bosnian evangelicals were divided along national lines. Otto's interaction with Samuil Petrovski, an evangelical student leader, led to MCC sponsorship of a conference for evangelical students from Serbia, Croatia, and other parts of former Yugoslavia. A small initiative, this conference was likely the first of its kind after the wars of the 1990s, one that also strengthened the awareness on the part of many evangelical leaders of the Christian call to peacemaking. The conference created ties of fellowship across former battle lines which have continued to this day.

work for outside audiences. Besides Pontanima, Face to Face conducted public events such as round tables where theologians or local religious leaders would share with each other about their religious traditions and think together about possible avenues of cooperation and collaboration. Face to Face worked with religious leaders to help cooperation between neighboring villages of differing religious backgrounds about cooperation in development projects. Face to Face seeks to connect religious leaders across national and religious boundaries, including building connections between visiting Western Christians and Serbian, Croatian, and Bosnian religious leaders. Fra. Marković, for example, highlights the importance of taking visiting religious leaders to meet the Serbian Orthodox priests in Pale close to Sarajevo. Fra. Marković believes bringing these groups, including Protestant leaders, together has been helped slowly familiarize the Orthodox priests with Protestant groups.

Another aspect of Face to Face's early work was educating visiting North Americans, both religious and secular leaders, about the region's religious heritage and the possibilities of co-existence. Amy Gopp described part of her assignment as inter-preting the political, religious, and cultural situation to out-siders. Through its usually well-received foreign performances, Pontanima serves, in the words of MCC worker Keziah Conrad, as an ambassador for interfaith cooperation and friendship, for what is good in Bosnia.

Not all Pontanima performances, however, are well received. Occasionally local performances have elicited hostile reactions, as during a performance around the time of the opening of the restored bridge in Mostar in 2004. While audiences scarred by interethnic and interreligious battles often respond with gratitude to Pontanima's embodiment of interfaith reconciliation, for some audiences the wounds are simply too fresh.

Keziah Conrad's work at Face to Face (2002-2006) continued MCC's support for the logistical, managerial, and fundraising tasks essential to the success of Pontanima's frequent concerts and tours. The choir's international recognition means that it travels internationally several times a year and gives frequent performances in Bosnia. Conrad also initiated a project to inter-view all choir members about what Pontanima means to them. The interviews were published as part of the choir's tenth anniversary celebration, held in June 2006. A recurring theme in these interviews is the importance of the choir for choir members as a community to which they belong.

Within Pontanima there is not much explicit discussion about religion or about the work of interfaith dialogue. Fra. Marković articulates the reasons and theology behind Pontanima's work in presentations during concerts, talking about how the choir is a place where interfaith connections are fostered. Some have suggested that choir members be invited to teach each other about their own religious traditions; this suggestion, however, has been set aside perhaps out of fear that the line between teaching about religion and preaching religion might be crossed.

The Face to Face initiative has served as an incubator for other interfaith peacebuilding initiatives. Fra. Marković highlights how Face to Face has collected positive stories of people helping each other during the war across religious lines and has contributed to connecting grassroots initiatives from differing religious backgrounds. Face to Face, Fra. Marković believes, is a motor for these other peacebuilding initiatives. Face to Face also has also led tours of the diverse places of worship in Sarajevo for over 1,000 children from other towns, has organized a televised annual interreligious prayer broadcast through the country, and operates a library with resources on religion and sacred music.

In addition to working in close partnership with interfaith initiatives like Face to Face and Pontanima, MCC has assisted the outreach of a Muslim charity network, Merhamet, by providing relief aid to Merhamet's soup kitchens. This organization operates as an umbrella for various separate humanitarian initiatives at the local and national level. MCC cooperated with Merhamet in Croatia in early relief projects through the Baptist outreach Duhovna Stvarnost.

Just as important as interfaith dialogue about beliefs, if not more so, is this type of interfaith cooperation to meet basic human needs. Shipping relief goods through a Muslim organization, although not a direct form of "interfaith dialogue," is a symbol of respect for another faith-based organization and community. Recent MCC plans have emphasized the importance of partnerships with organizations such as Merhamet as expressions of MCC's commitment to a gospel of peace.

Bridge-building work in Serbia, 1996-2005

During the same period that MCC was establishing partnerships with Face to Face and Pontanima, MCC continued to place workers in Serbia. MCC's work in Serbia unfolded against the backdrop of the international sanctions regime in place over Serbia and Montenegro from 1992 to 2000. Many Serbians did not view MCC workers from Canada and the United States as neutral but as outsiders from hostile countries that had placed Serbia under economic siege. The U.S.-led bombing of Bosnian Serb positions in 1995 and attacks on Serbian police and military targets in 1999 during the war in Kosovo exacerbated this perception of MCC workers, especially those from the United States. MCC issued statements during this period denouncing the bombing, even though the stated intention of the bombing campaign was to protect civilians.

Nevertheless, MCC workers, like other foreigners, particularly from the West, found that living in Serbia during this time was challenging, given the antagonisms between Serbia and the NATO alliance. MCC's continued placement of workers in Serbia embodied the Mennonite conviction that the church must stand separate from the military and the state. MCC was one of the few international organizations with expatriate personnel in Serbia.

MCC volunteers were also involved in fostering interfaith bridge building, although in a less formal way. Harold Otto, MCC worker from 1996-1999, worked to encourage Serbian evangelicals to be more open to encounters with other faith understandings. Otto also focused on developing relationships within the Serbian Orthodox Church. Thanks to Otto, MCC also began working with Marijana Ajzenkol, an active participant in the seminars for mid-level religious leaders conducted by the Center for Strategic and International Studies, which grew out of the ecumenical workshop that Gerald Shenk had organized. Otto encouraged Ajzenkol in her vision of establishing a Serbian-based organization dedicated to addressing interfaith matters. The vision became reality with the founding of the Interreligious Center.

The Interreligious Center seeks to foster long-term relationships among clerics from different faith traditions. More important to Ajzenkol than statements of tolerance signed by religious

ANALYZING MCC'S INTERFAITH
COMMITMENTS IN SOUTHEAST EUROPE

As this brief history of MCC's experience in southeast Europe has shown, Mennonites have been privileged to walk alongside persons from diverse faith communities in a war-torn region as they have sought to build interfaith bridges across religious divides. Some common themes and issues run through MCC's work in the varied contexts of Serbia, Bosnia, Croatia, and other parts of the former Yugoslavia, themes and issues that perhaps illuminate the challenges and promise of MCC's interfaith work worldwide.

Contribution of MCC

The bridge-building work described here was mostly carried out by local individuals and actors. MCC has sought to strengthen the work of people who will continue peacebuilding and community development work long after international support has dried up. MCC's role has not always been publicly visible; the partner organization plans and executes the project, with MCC support remaining in the background.

A word to describe MCC's interfaith work that arose in interviews for this chapter was *non-impositional* (or *nenametljivi*). A recent report released by the U.S. Institute of Peace emphasizes the benefits of long-term approaches in peacebuilding work, the vital significance of extended commitment to developing relationships and of empowering local initiatives. The USIP report highlights the work of the Pontanima choir as exemplary of a long-term, grassroots peacebuilding approach. MCC's work in southeast Europe has, at its best, been about cultivating long-term relationships and, in the context of these relationships, encouraging and supporting the visions of Serbian, Croatian, Bosnian, and other partners.[5]

Fra. Marković emphasizes the importance of MCC in resourcing the church and other organizations with materials on the gospel of nonviolence. Gerald Shenk presented books on Mennonite theology to Fra. Marković, who then translated and distributed them within the Bosnian Franciscan community. Fra. Marković has been struck by what he sees as the overlap between Mennonite and Franciscan theology. He observes that

MCC workers have been a source of spiritual support to peace workers in the region such as himself who are at times isolated and criticized within their own faith communities.

Marijana Ajzenkol of the Interreligious Center concurs, emphasizing the importance of the physical presence of MCC workers. MCC support is not from afar, but emerges from lived relationships. Living in the region, Mennonite workers develop cultural and linguistic skills indispensable for effective peace work. By being present in the culture, furthermore, MCC workers build friendships with ordinary believers from different faith traditions, not only connections with high-level religious leaders.

In many cases, MCC is one of the few financial supporters of interfaith bridge-building efforts like Face to Face, Pontanima, and the Interreligious Center. In an environment in which raising financial support locally is difficult, international support is crucial. However, few international donors have the long-term perspective to foster local initiatives. Although the amounts are often not large, local organizations often lack the linguistic and cultural knowledge to access foreign funds. Many foreign donors also lack a commitment to interfaith bridge building. MCC thus helps fill in a significant funding gap.

Theology

MCC conducts its work as a representative of Mennonite and Brethren in Christ churches in the U.S. and Canada. When I interviewed current and former MCC workers about how their interfaith engagement has affected their own faith, they reported sensing that some Mennonites feared their interfaith engagements would weaken or dilute their faith. Instead, the MCC workers with whom I spoke stressed that their faith had been strengthened through interfaith collaboration and interaction.

MCC workers I interviewed talked about how through their assignments they had developed an awareness that God is at work in other religious traditions, a conviction that Jesus did not build walls around the Christian community. Conversion, they observed, is something that comes from God, not from humans. MCC workers have thus been more concerned about embodying the boundary-breaking reality of the gospel than actively seeking to convert others. Workers described befriending people of other religious traditions as a form of witness to the Christian faith, an embodiment of the theology that through Jesus God has befriended all of humanity. MCC workers point to the ministry of Pontanima as an example of such interfaith community-building and friendship-forming. The sacred songs of Pontanima invite people to dwell in the presence of God, to look forward to a deeper, spiritual, peace, a peace greater than the simple absence of war.

Many MCC workers and MCC partners in southeast Europe note that their encounters with persons from other religious of those interviewed groups have affected them deeply, showing them the beauty and interconnectedness of diverse faiths. Such an awareness has a lasting impact. For Marijana Ajzenkol, the healthy faith of someone outside her own faith community supports her own faith. For several people I interviewed, daily interactions with Muslims have been important for deconstructing post-9-11 stereotypes of Islam and of Muslims. MCC workers regularly share their positive experiences with Muslim neighbors and co-workers with their home congregations, thus further helping to dispel misconceptions and prejudices.

The Impact of Interfaith Work

Search for Common Ground, a U.S. non-governmental organization active in conflict resolution and peacebuilding work, has recognized the Pontanima choir as an innovative approach to doing interfaith bridge building.[6] Pontanima's music touches the core of people in a way that is hard to put into words. Pontanima's performances throughout Bosnia routinely move audience and choir members alike to tears. Having members of other ethnic groups sing solos from the music of other ethnic and faith traditions has been particularly powerful, as it demonstrates respect for the other tradition and religion and thus contributes to healing. Pontanima's performs without analysis or theology; this, former MCC worker Karin Kaufman Wall believes, has contributed to its effectiveness. MCC worker Keziah Conrad highlights the unifying power of individuals singing together as a single organism and also stresses that through Pontanima's performances a prophetic truth about co-existence and reconciliation is embodied and articulated.

MCC workers and partners who were interviewed spoke of the general openness in North America to hear of their work. Pontanima has toured twice in the United States, including visits to Mennonite communities. In both tours, for the most part, Pontanima experienced a warm open reception from Mennonite communities. Kaufman Wall suggests that this openness to Pontanima's message of interfaith cooperation can be attributed in part to Mennonite appreciation for the arts, especially song. At the same time, however, MCC workers facilitating Pontanima tours sometimes noticed a subtle pressure from MCC and from Mennonite communities in North America to tone down stories of interfaith dialogue for fear such stories will be viewed as theologically suspect.

FRAMEWORKS FOR UNDERSTANDING INTERFAITH BRIDGE BUILDING IN SOUTHEAST EUROPE

Former MCC Area Director for Europe Hansulrich Gerber describes the development of MCC's interfaith programs in southeast Europe as organic developments driven by the neighborly and collegial relationships developed by MCC workers in their differing contexts. Put theologically, one could say that MCC has sought to be open to the movement of God's Spirit as the Spirit has led MCC into a deeper and wider network of ecumenical and interfaith relationships.

The study *Interfaith Dialogue and Peacebuilding* articulates a helpful framework for understanding interfaith dialogue.[7] The study advocates an approach which denies the existence of a global religious conflict and instead emphasizes the religious dimensions of local conflicts and the potential of religion and religious actors to contribute to building peace. Drawing on an approach formulated by Leonard Swidler, this framework delineates three types of interreligious dialogue and interaction: "the practical, where we collaborate to help humanity; the depth of 'spiritual' dimension, where we attempt to experience the partners' religion or ideology 'from within'; the cognitive, where we seek understanding [of] the truth."

MCC's interfaith work in southeast Europe has mostly involved the first and second dimensions identified by Swidler.

The second, "spiritual," dimension is embodied both in initiatives like Pontanima and the Interreligious Center and in the lived experiences of MCC workers who build friendships with persons from a wide variety of other religious traditions. The first, or "practical," approach is exemplified by MCC's cooperation with the Muslim organization, Merhamet, in its work to help refugees and low-income families meet basic human needs.

MCC-supported interfaith initiatives have worked with both the grassroots and the leadership levels. MCC has not emphasized organizing seminars in which high-level religious leaders draft statements about tolerance or co-existence or engage in detailed theological dialogue about doctrinal convergence or divergence. Instead, MCC-supported projects have placed a premium on the creation of community and relationships over a long period of time. Dialogue about beliefs and doctrines takes a back seat to fostering relationships across religious divides.

Mennonite conflict transformation practitioner John Paul Lederach emphasizes the importance of relationships in the process of reconciliation.[8] Groups like Pontanima, Face to Face, and the Interreligious Center share with Lederach the conviction that the cultivation of relationships across fields of difference is essential for reconciliation. These organizations bring people together to experience fellowship with one another. The being of fellowship is more important for these initiatives than the "doing" of particular projects.

Sally Engle Merry suggests that Mennonite peacebuilding efforts are characterized by two key features: leaving control in the hands of local parties and an emphasis on grassroots participation.[9] Mennonite interfaith peacebuilding commitments in southeast Europe bear out Merry's analysis. Merry also identifies key terms and practices from Mennonite peacebuilding work worldwide, including the importance of witness and presence, following the lead of partners and not seeking control of projects, a commitment to long-term presence, an emphasis on working from the edge (in the sense of working with marginalized individuals and organizations), and entry into conflict settings through relationship-building.

MCC's experience in southeast Europe, however, doesn't always fit Merry's analytical framework. Merry's analysis emphasizes the understanding of peacebuilding as a part of social justice work and confronting social inequality. MCC's interfaith work in southeast Europe, however, has tended not to emphasize justice-seeking but rather building relationships on all "sides," then supporting efforts at reconciliation emerging from those contexts.

On the whole, however, Merry's description of Mennonite peace work worldwide captures well the nature of Mennonite interfaith bridge building in the former Yugoslavia. The similarity between Mennonite interfaith work and peacebuilding work should be no surprise, as Mennonite involvements in interfaith matters, at least in southeast Europe, is driven in large part by an understanding of how religion has contributed to horrific violence and a desire to see how religion might be used as a source of peacebuilding.

Interfaith bridge building is hard to measure according to the language of goals, objectives, and indicators. As MCC, like other relief and development agencies, becomes more immersed in the language of results-based management and in quantifying progress, the language of "presence" and "standing with" partners slowly falls out of favor.

However, one might suggest that it has been through the presence of MCC workers in the varied contexts of southeast Europe, through the relationships they have built, that MCC can claim to have contributed to "results" in the realm of interfaith bridge building. MCC presence led to relationships with people like Fra. Marković and Marijana Ajzenkol. This in turn led to support of initiatives like Pontanima and the Interreligious Center, both of which have influenced members of the top leadership in Bosnia and Serbia.

The impact of MCC-supported projects often takes years to be seen. MCC's experience in southeast Europe thus suggests that if one is (rightly) concerned about results in interfaith bridge building, one must be prepared to invest time and personnel resources in the relationships that will make up the bridge.

NOTES

1. Interviews were conducted with current and former MCC workers Keziah Conrad, Hansulrich Gerber, Amy Gopp, Karin Kaufman

Wall, Harold Otto, and MCC partners Marijana Ajzenkol and Fra. Ivo Marković.

2. Misha Glenny, *The Fall of Yugoslavia: The Third Balkan War* (London: Penguin, 1992), 111.

3. Gerald Shenk, *God With Us? The Roles of Religion in Conflicts in the Former Yugoslavia* (Uppsala, Sweden: Life and Peace Institute, 1993).

4. David Steele, "Peacebuilding in the Former Yugoslavia," in *Interfaith Dialogue and Peacebuilding*, ed. David R. Smock (Washington, D.C.: U.S. Institute of Peace, 2002).

5. United States Institute of Peace, *Can Faith-Based NGOs Advance Interfaith Reconciliation: The Case of Bosnia-Herzegovina* (Washington, D,C.: U.S. Institute of Peace, 2003).

6. More information is available at www.sfcg.org/sfcg/sfcg_awards 2004.html.

7. David R. Smock, ed. *Interfaith Dialogue and Peacebuilding* (Washington, D.C.: U.S. Institute of Peace, 2002).

8. John Paul Lederach, *Building Peace: Sustainable Reconciliation in Divided Societies* (Washington, D.C.: U.S. Institute of Peace, 1997).

9. Sally Engle Merry, "Mennonite Peacebuilding and Conflict Transformation: A Cultural Analysis," in *From the Ground Up: Mennonite Contributions to International Peacebuilding*, ed. Cynthia Sampson and John Paul Lederach (New York: Oxford University Press, 2002).

Chapter 10

Who Owns Jesus? Interfaith Connections in India

Jon Rudy

Some years ago, a quiet Indian Muslim man, a recipient of assistance from Mennonite Central Committee (MCC), asked an MCC India worker, "Did Jesus come for Christians only?" At one stage of her life, the MCC worker might have answered differently. But because of internalized gospel values nurtured by MCC, she responded, "No, he came for me and you. He had a humble birth."

Those who have worked with MCC for many years have had these simple questions permeate their lives. The challenge of living as a minority Christian in India, where there are more shades of gray than in the afternoon storm clouds, forms into the question, "Who owns Jesus?" Do Christians have exclusive claims on understanding Christ and interpreting his work in the world today? When an MCC worker, a Christian whose husband is Hindu, observes, "We have a lot of discussions [on issues of faith], me and my husband, but he believes in Jesus," how do we understand this claim theologically?

MCC has had a long and fruitful presence in India. MCC currently employs a relatively large Indian staff; programmatically, MCC provides small community development grants, supports peace initiatives, and engages and emergency relief responses. In this chapter I will describe some of the projects supported by MCC India that involve and nurture interfaith collaboration. These initiatives in turn spur theological reflection about the challenges posed by interfaith work. I conclude this chapter by reflecting on the theological implications of MCC India's interfaith work.

MCC INDIA: SITTING
TOGETHER AND HEARING ONE ANOTHER

One cannot be in India long and ignore the dizzying religious plurality of this subcontinent. Religion is everywhere, made most visible by the numerous Hindu shrines and Muslim mosques dotting the land and cityscapes. Christianity is a minority religion in India. By and large different faiths live together in harmony and peace, yet all too often the social pressures bred by poverty and structural injustice explode in localized communal violence.

Often the most convenient dividing line in open conflict is religion. An interreligious confrontation in one area of the country has repercussions throughout India. In a country in which sectarian violence can be whipped up with the ferocity of the monsoon rains, building interfaith bridges is a critical element of sustainable development and violence prevention amid disadvantaged multi-religious communities.

While MCC's work in India began in response to the Bengal famine in 1942, material aid and relief distributions have gradually yielded within the MCC India program to a focus on development and peace. Major catastrophes, like the December 2004 tsunami, still, of course, prompt relief responses by MCC. MCC has also responded with humanitarian assistance in the wake of communal violence that occasionally erupts along religious fault lines.

In responding to a natural disaster, be it cyclone, drought, or tsunami, MCC has tried to leverage its assistance to have a longer-term impact that lessens the vulnerability of affected communities to further disasters. Vulnerability mitigation is also a goal of MCC's response to human-made disasters such as sectarian violence. To reduce the likelihood of future violence, MCC supports conflict transformation workshops in such cases alongside aid intervention. Not surprisingly, then, conversations across religious lines have been an inevitable offshoot of meeting human need in India. Within the multi-religious milieu of India, MCC's sensitivity to other faiths has matured.

Connecting with a wide array of community leaders as part of their relief, development, and peacebuilding work, MCC's Indian staff, predominantly Christians, come into daily contact with Hindus, Muslims, and persons of other faiths. This interaction has stimulated a transformation of faith values for both MCC's local Indian staff and MCC service workers from North America alike. One MCC staff person observed that when church persons "tangle" with persons from other faiths, they learn through the give-and-take of daily life to know and love those people.

Personal examples of transformation abound. As one staff member described learnings regarding persons of other faiths, "Since working for MCC my whole outlook has changed."[1] Looking back at MCC history, another MCC India worker noted, "Thirty-seven years ago there was more emphasis on directly enunciating our faith, but now it is more indirect, by bringing people together, seeing the commonalities in a learning posture." This gradual change in outlook has created some difficulties for staff as they continue to work with churches whose focus is conversion of non-Christians. "The more church people connect with the people whose religious persuasions they are trying to change, the more they might discover their answers from the Bible are not so black and white," noted one staff member. "Faith . . . is coming to awareness of others," stated another.

MCC India's answer to the question of who owns Jesus starts with the understanding that the way Jesus lived his life embodies the fullness of God's love, a love that is immeasurably embracing. The uniquely Christian message is about the wideness of God's love and mercy, an abundant gift to be shared, not a scarce commodity to be hoarded. By guarding the message, we've made God too small. In reality there is a wideness in God's kingdom.

At the same time, and somewhat paradoxically, MCC India stresses the need to respect differences. "We have not sold our soul to the devil when we don't always always always talk Jesus Jesus Jesus, salvation, heaven and hell, and all that stuff," asserts one MCC India staff member. "I am not going to insist that everyone use exactly the same words I use."

A third understanding of MCC India staff is that true dialogue happens among equals. It is, says one MCC worker, "two equals sitting together and genuinely hearing each other. It is not something special I bring to you." Another claims, "To find a common denominator is not a dilution, but a broader perspective on God's love and being God's children."

Finally, MCC India staff workers recognize the role of the Holy Spirit in interfaith collaboration. "We don't know how the Spirit works. We don't know whom the Spirit touches, and we will never know because it is something we don't control. We are not in charge of this. It's the Spirit that responds, not your intellect, in dialogue."

The overarching programmatic philosophy of MCC India might be described, in the words of one staff member, as "everything we do is to bring people together." So when MCC workers discuss the values they bring to meeting human need in the name of Christ, they use words like *participatory, relational, holistic,* and *impartial* (with reference to caste and religion). They say faith is demonstrated by accepting persons as persons, taking time with people, showing Christ-inspired love for them. MCC India's values and programmatic approaches in turn influence what partnerships MCC India initiates. MCC India has been fortunate to join in the ministries of Indian organizations that embody a dialogical spirit of bridge building across interfaith divides. In what follows I describe the work of two such organizations: St. Mary's Mahila Shikshan Kendra and the Henry Martyn Institute.

EMERGENCY RESPONSE THROUGH ST. MARY'S MAHILA SHIKSHAN KENDRA

In 2002 in Ahmedabad, Gujarat State, violence between Hindus and Muslims erupted. The violence was sparked on February 27, when Hindu activists returning from a pilgrimage were attacked by a Muslim mob after their train stopped at the town of Godhra. Some reports claim the Hindus may have taken food without paying Muslim vendors at previous stops. When they reached Godhra, angry Muslims on the platform, possibly incited by unidentified provocateurs, set fire to the train. Fifty-nine people, many of them women, died. In the wake of the attack on the train, Hindus in Gujarat began a massacre of Muslims in many neighborhoods. In the end, 2,500 people were killed in the riots, and more than 11,000 homes were destroyed.

The Dominican Sisters' compound in Ahmedabad became an oasis of peace during the riots, with many Muslims crowded within their flimsy walls. The sisters asked those Muslim familes who had fled to the convent if they were sure they wanted to be there, because the nuns couldn't physically protect the Muslims from the rampaging Hindu mobs if the convent came under attack. The Muslim families replied: "This is holy ground, and we would rather die together." Anyone could have entered the compound to drag the Muslims out, but no one came in because, notes an MCC India worker, "these women had been in the community for years, and everyone knew they didn't play favorites." Christians like the Dominican sisters became trusted third parties during these sectarian riots.

MCC India's directors hesitated at first to become involved in providing relief assistance in response to this situation due to its political nature and its distance from most MCC India project areas. MCC's Indian staff, however, urged MCC to respond in some way. The rioting demonstrated some of the "most ugly acts, and we Christians were made aware that this fundamentalism has to be fought together with other faiths" said an MCC staff member.

MCC decided to support the work of St. Mary's Mahila Shikshan Kendra, a women's group run by Catholic Dominican sisters near a Muslim neighborhood in Ahmedabad. Since MCC already had a relationship with this women's group through the Ten Thousand Villages fair trade organization, it was a natural place to look for ways to serve. Rebuilding housing destroyed in the riots was a natural response. MCC began by providing funds to rebuild the women's group staff homes that had been destroyed. Later, MCC helped to rebuild an additional 102 houses. Through this emergency reconstruction response, MCC India joined the outreach of an Indian Christian organization in a healing ministry amid a community wounded by interfaith divides.

PEACEBUILDING TRAINING
THROUGH THE HENRY MARTYN INSTITUTE

The Henry Martyn Institute (HMI) owes its name to an Anglican missionary who was a chaplain of the East India Company in the early 1800s. In his short life (1781-1812), Martyn mastered sixteen languages and translated the New Testament into Urdu, Arabic, and Persian. Samuel Zwemer, a missionary from the United States, was the driving force behind the founding of HMI as a project of the Indian National Council of Churches in 1930. Initially located in what is present-day Lahore, Pakistan, HMI began with a mandate to undertake a variety of research and translation projects meant to foster "dialogue with Muslim communities as part of their [HMI's] mission of evangelization."[2] HMI is today located in the city of Hyderabad, in the Indian state of Andhra Pradesh. Situated on a beautiful campus on the outskirts of the city, it is currently known for its work at interfaith academic studies and offers theological degrees in Islamic studies. It has one of the most extensive Islamic libraries in India.

After a consultation connected with its golden anniversary in 1990, HMI shifted its focus from support for the evangelization of Muslims to reconciliation. The impetus for and confirmation of this shift came with the Hindu-Muslim sectarian violence that rocked Hyderabad in the 1980s and again in 1990 and 1992. Beyond academic programs offering diplomas and degrees on Islam and related languages, HMI staff looked for ways to address this community crisis. The result was a series of community development workshops, conflict resolution and peacebuilding programs, and a women's interfaith exchange program with an emphasis on practical initiatives involving women from different religious backgrounds. All work at HMI is "directed toward the same goal of bringing people together, building relationships which will help HMI in transforming the structures of communalism and differences."[3]

Because of this shift in HMI's programmatic mandate, some Christian groups that continue to work actively at converting Muslims resent HMI. The sentiment from some Christians has been that "there's something wrong with this approach, it is not Christian," noted one MCC India worker. HMI work, she observed, is not about "who is going to convert who, but [about] two religions coming together in a beautiful way."

Mennonites have been involved in providing resources for the HMI institutional paradigm shift. In 1992, Katharine Fairfield conducted a two-day conflict resolution workshop at HMI sponsored by MCC. In the late 1990s, Ron Kraybill of Eastern Mennonite University's Center for Justice and Peace spent a year assisting HMI in setting up their diploma course in conflict studies. In 2001 and 2002, HMI staff received training at the MCC-supported Mindanao Peacebuilding Institute in the Philippines. Several MCC India staff members, meanwhile, have participated in workshops offered by the HMI conflict resolution/peacebuilding program. MCC workers have also served on HMI's board of directors.

One HMI community program aimed at reducing interfaith tensions in the Hyderabad area is in the slum of Sultan Shahi, where HMI has a community building called Aman Shanti (the word peace in both Urdu and Hindi languages). The building is directly positioned between Muslim and Hindu communities. This center contains a clinic, a skills training workshop for women, and a pre-school for children of different faiths. At first the Muslim and Hindu women who used the center didn't interact with each other. Gradually, however, through daily involvement in the Aman Shanti programs, these women began to celebrate each other's festivals, get to know each other as sisters, and overcome their prejudices.

At a recent conference sponsored by HMI focusing on interfaith conversations, staff members articulated their understandings of dialogue. "Our conference is animated by the conviction that religious traditions have to collaborate and take joint responsibility on the local, national, and international levels for the future of the world by working toward a more just world order, where matters relating to peace are of the essence," shared one HMI worker. Another HMI staff member explained that

> For the past fifteen years a dedicated team of workers has been trying to put out the raging fires of communal hatred and violent conflicts through its various programs: the academic work, teaching about Islam and interfaith relations, the praxis work, working among different religious communities in the poorer areas of our city, and the conflict resolution workshops in various conflict ridden parts of our country. The HMI team has been like the hummingbird

pouring water drop by drop to heal the wounds of hatred, of division, of anger.[4]

THEOLOGICAL REFLECTION

MCC India's partnerships with the Henry Martyn Institute and St. Mary's Mahila Shikshan Kendra grow out of MCC's International Program Department's core values, specifically the value of *relationship building*. As an MCC key initiative, interfaith bridge building takes a variety of forms, but always with an emphasis on relationships. Ed Martin, MCC's Area Director for South and Central Asia, calls the interfaith bridge-building approach used most often by MCC workers and programs a "dialogue of the village," in which MCC workers simply live, interact, and are present in diverse religious situations. He continues, "The conversations around tea are almost more fruitful than papers presented during a conference." In MCC India's interfaith work, relationships have been key. Doctrinal differences have been secondary to the imperative of responding to human needs, especially needs identified amid interfaith relationships.

MCC India's interfaith work has developed out of the organization-wide mandate of sharing the "cold cup of water" and the belief that actions speak louder than words about the nature of God's kingdom. This approach generates numerous starting points for interfaith conversations. Connecting across religious divides, be they interfaith or ecumenical, embodies an inherently *inclusive* gospel. By ever widening the circle of relationships, MCC demonstrates that all persons are children of God.

Putting programmatic feet to MCC's core values in interfaith contexts does not typically involve MCC in direct dialogue; rather, MCC is heavily involved through its partners in *supporting* dialogue initiatives. This is true in India but also throughout Asia and beyond. These local initiatives are what one MCC India worker calls "islands of hope" in the region. Peacebuilding and conflict resolution institutes in Asia supported by MCC (including the HMI, the Mindanao Peacebuilding Institute, and new initiatives such as the Annual Peacebuilding and Reconciliation Program in Luzon, Philippines) stimulate participants to think about what programmatic ways can be developed to forge and nurture interfaith friendship and collaboration.

Interfaith transformation poses challenges for those living in communities not necessarily supportive of interfaith ventures. "You have to keep a separation between your own philosophy and MCC's because it may not represent MCC," lamented one MCC India worker. The staff person spoke of incongruity between on the one hand what MCC staffers experience in their churches and understand some of MCC's supporting churches in Canada and the United States to believe and, on the other hand, how they personally have walked the path of dialogue while working for MCC. Inclusiveness may bridge gaps in one place while creating rifts in others. "You may create a problem in the church by how you think and express that process of dialogue," observes one MCC India staff member. To move out in dialogue may bring challenge from within Christian circles. "We need support and cooperation to be united. . . . We could do so much more if we were all united. We are so fragmented and have our own little kingdoms," stressed one worker.

Internal differences in the Christian community are as acute and in need of mending as the rifts between different faiths. MCC India does not seek to "plant the Mennonite flag" in the Indian context. It is therefore strategically placed to relate to a wide variety of Christian groups and build human bridges between them.

By moving toward relational gaps and inhabiting those gaps, we find the norms of our faith challenged. "Who owns Jesus?" asks a Muslim man in India. Transformation happens as we grapple with questions such as these.

NOTES

1. Quotations from MCC India staff are all from a September 15, 2005 interview by the author with MCC India workers at the MCC India office in Kolkata, West Bengal, India. Present in the interview were five program workers with more than 100 years of combined experience working with MCC. It is at the staff's request that individuals are not named in this article.

2. Lakshmi Raman, *A Spiritual Harvest: Evaluation of HMI from the Period of 1999 to 2003* (Bangalore, India: Kaizen Surya Associates, June 7, 2004), 5.

3. *A Spiritual Harvest*, 57.

4. "Drop by Drop: Building a Community," from a Conference on Interfaith Collaboration (Dec. 5-7, 2005).

Chapter 11

A Theology
of Interfaith Bridge
Building

Peter Dula

*R*om Coles begins his book, *Self/Power/Other*, with a citation
from Barry Lopez's *Arctic Dreams*. Lopez is among the greatest of
American "nature writers." In his work over the last thirty years
he has graciously and generously inhabited the borderlands between human and non-human. The citation Coles chooses concerns borderlands, the borderlands ecologists calls "ecotones."
Ecotones are the borders between two different ecological communities, say between a wood and a meadow. Ecologists know
that those borders "often harbor a greater variety and density of
life" than either the forest or the grassland alone. Lopez calls
them "special meeting grounds" and says that "the mingling of
animals from different ecosystems charges such border zones
with evolutionary potential."[1]

Coles uses these ecotones as an image for borders that have
long been the concern of political philosophy: between cultures,
self and other, black and white, male and female, religions, and
more. Coles takes off from this to note that

> Western civilization has a long and dark history with re-
> spect to edges; it tends to view them as indicative of an evil

160

that lies on the other side; it constitutes them as regions to be forever thrust back and ultimately eliminated at the moment when we conquer the other.[2]

Western civilization has often turned the borderlands into spaces of desolation instead of fecundity. But what if we, as Mennonites and as an organization like Mennonite Central Committee, dwelled in these ecotones in hope instead of fear? What if MCC chose to inhabit these regions in the knowledge that here is where creativity, growth, and what the church calls reformation happen? What if MCC chose to inhabit the borderlands not because it has joined the liberals and secularists in doubting the truth of Christ, but precisely because of its unshakable conviction in Christ's lordship? What if MCC chose to transform the threat of otherness into opportunity, refusing to be controlled by fear?

What I will try to show in these remarks is that Karl Barth is one of the best theological guides to how to confront these challenges, how to live in hope and expectation in the borderlands. Specifically, I believe that the section of Barth's *Church Dogmatics* called "The Light of Life," a subsection of Barth's treatment of Christ's prophetic office, provides valuable theological insights into life in the borderlands.[3] This chapter aims first to show, via Barth, that engaging persons of other faiths hospitably is an imperative for Christians; and second, to provide some guidelines for doing so.

Part of Barth's achievement, as we will see, is his disruption of the categories usually invoked in discussions of interfaith matters—exclusivism, inclusivism, pluralism. It may nevertheless be helpful to briefly sketch those alternatives as a background to Barth's position. Liberal views tend to be roughly Kantian. That is, liberals tend to see all religions are equally true. To support such a view, they tend to treat religions in a reductionist manner. Differences and incompatibilities between religions are recognized but understood as inessential—there is, in this view, an essential core shared by all religions which can be seen once the historical and practical accretions are stripped away. Tolerance is commendable, because deep down we are all the same. Both the so-called "pluralist" and "inclusivist" approaches to religious diversity tend to replicate this basic Kantian approach.

The conservative view is usually some kind of exclusivism. Strictly speaking, exclusivism means that "true religious claims are found only among the doctrines and teachings of [one's own] religion."[4] Outside of, say, Christianity, there can be no truth. That, however, is a purely theoretical position which it is hard to imagine anyone actually believing. There is simply too much overlap among Christianity, Islam, and Judaism, or among Hinduism, Buddhism, and Jainism, for example. More common is a modified exclusivist view that while other religions may know some truths, they know far fewer truths than Christianity and, most importantly, none the Christian doesn't already know.

While the liberal Kantian approach and the conservative exclusivist approach may seem like polar opposites, they share one crucial thing in common. Both views preclude the possibility of ecotones. The liberal view has no need to engage difference because in the end there is no difference. Deep down we are all the same. The conversations in which liberals engage are guaranteed never to become too threatening. The conservatives also have no need to engage difference since they already know whatever the other might have to teach.

The situation is rather different for Barth. "We must now go on to make an emphasis," Barth writes, "which is decisive for our understanding of the whole. In other words, we must make a conscious because necessary application of the definite article. Jesus Christ is *the* light of life" (86). Jesus Christ is the one and only light in all fullness and perfection. There is no other light outside or alongside this person. "There are," he says, "horses which will constantly shy at this hurdle and think they must refuse it" (87), but we cannot and must not do so.

Barth realizes that his stand will generate strenuous protest from a number of different corners. He outlines the protest in some detail. The claim that Jesus Christ is *the* light of life is arrogant, presumptuous, capricious. Intellectually it is "obscurantist" and severely narrows the field of inquiry. Morally and politically, it destroys relationships, fosters intolerance, and creates the conditions from which arise crusades and witch trials. Moreover, it is not just the non-Christians or the liberal theologians who will say this. In us too, Barth confesses, there will always be an inner voice telling us the same thing. The criticism hits home because we all share it at some level (89–90).

All these objections and temptations notwithstanding, "we have no option in this matter." Christian freedom "stands or falls by whether it is freedom for this confession" (90). Therefore we must make this confession as boldly as possible, but first we had better make sure we are clear about what it means. Barth is convinced that we haven't been clear enough; therefore objections to strong christological claims are based on a "supreme misunderstanding." Just in case you are hoping or fearing that Barth is now going to relax the exclusiveness of the statement to make it more inclusive and tolerant, he, as usual, does the opposite. He intensifies the exclusiveness.

> The statement that Jesus Christ is the one Word of God has really nothing whatever to do with the arbitrary exaltation and self-glorification of the Christian in relation to other men, of the church in relation to other institutions, or of Christianity in relation to other conceptions.
>
> It is a christological statement. It looks away from non-Christian and Christian alike to the One who sovereignly confronts and precedes both as *the* prophet. . . . Thus the criticism expressed in the exclusiveness of the statement affects, limits and relativises the prophecy of Christians and the Church no less than the many other prophecies, lights and words. (91)

Barth goes on to expand upon what this statement does not say. If the referent of the statement "Jesus Christ is the one Word of God" is Jesus Christ, then the "one Word of God" is not anything else. First, it is not Scripture. Of course, Barth is very careful about how he says this, having in mind the particular kinds of appeals made to *sola scriptura* by fundamentalists, or Lutherans of the more vulgar type. The "one Word of God" is also not the church. Here Barth has in mind primarily, but not only, certain Roman Catholic appeals to "tradition" and "authority." There are certainly true words and true lights in this sphere, but "these lights shine only because of the shining of none other light than His" (96). The revelation of God in Christ is total and complete. It doesn't need a supplement—Christ doesn't need help. (But we do.) "It is not His fault if we see and know so little of God and ourselves" (100). (But it is our fault.)

Moreover, it does not follow from the statement that Jesus is *the* light of life, "that every word spoken outside the circle of the

Bible and the Church is a word of false prophecy and therefore valueless, empty, and corrupt, that all the lights which rise and shine in this outer sphere [by outer sphere Barth means outside of the church] are misleading and all the revelations necessarily untrue" (97). If Christ is truly Lord, if "in him all things in heaven and on earth were created," if "all things have been created through him and for him . . . and in him all things hold together" (Col. 1.16-17), then it only makes sense that there is nowhere, not even the mouth of an ass, that we cannot expect to find words reflecting the light of the Word. There is, we might say, only one sun, but many moons, often in unexpected places.

I want to pause here briefly to unpack this. Barth is not advancing what he calls "the sorry hypothesis" of natural theology, the idea that knowledge of God arrives through reason's examination of the world. Natural theology presumed the possibility of acquiring knowledge of God independently of the specificity of Christ. Barth certainly believes that all creation proclaims the glory of God and that knowledge of God is attainable by observing creation (he is hesitant about calling it "nature"), but like Augustine and Calvin before him, Barth contends that one must observe creation through the lens of Christ, the one light. In other words, for Barth there is no doctrine of creation without the cross. Creation and redemption must be thought together.

I say all this to make one important point—that the separation of creation and redemption is not just a mistake of liberal theology. To "conservatively" rule out any revelation from creation makes the identical mistake of liberal theology. Both presume a separation between creation and redemption. They just read it differently.

There are true lights and words outside of Christ and the church. This necessarily follows from the freedom and lordship of Christ as well as from a proper doctrine of creation. It also follows that they cannot be allowed to crowd Christ out, to compete with him or replace him. All they can do is witness to him: "The living Lord Jesus Christ, risen again from the dead, has no serious rival as the one Prophet of God who does not merely attest to but is the Word of God" (100).

So we have our first criterion for whether another word is true—it witnesses to the one Word. It will only be a true word if

Christ the Word brings "Himself into the closest conjunction with such words" (101). Nothing can prevent him from doing so—even words outside the sphere of the Bible and the church can be made by the Word into witnesses to the Word. No words become witnesses to the Word on their own. No amount of striving and yearning can accomplish it. If it happens, it happens because of the power of Christ to draw them to him.

To commit oneself to the practice of interfaith bridge building is to presume, with Barth, that there are true lights and words in other religions. The point of interfaith bridge building is to see and listen to these true lights and words. But two questions remain. Even if there are such words and lights, why bother with them? If we are to engage them, how?

To the first: I presume that the motivation behind forging interfaith relationships is a desire to seek out and attend to the true lights and words beyond the walls of the church. But, one might ask, if Christ is *the* light, and all the others only reflections, why not just concentrate on Christ and leave the others aside? Perhaps they are worth pondering when we trip over them—but why actively seek them out? Barth's discussion of Christ the light of life suggests some pointed responses to these objections to interfaith bridge building.

First, Barth would probably be suspicious of this line of questioning. If all things visible and invisible are in Christ, if the doctrine of creation is a subset of the doctrine of redemption, then any rigid disjunction between the one Word and the words becomes theologically problematic. Attending to other words and lights is, on Barth's grounds, the way to focus on Christ.

Second, Barth has too low an opinion of Christians to trust us to attend to Christ well. He asks, "Can [the Church] ever pay sufficient attention to this one Word?" At first, this might sound like the question raised a paragraph ago: Why shouldn't we focus exclusively on Christ? But in the sentences immediately following, Barth turns the church's gaze beyond its walls: "Can it be content to hear it only from Holy Scripture and then from its own lips and tongue? Should it not be grateful to receive it also from without, in very different human words, in a secular parable?" (115).

Barth, unlike any theologian I am familiar with, except for John Howard Yoder and Rowan Williams, never let up on the re-

166 *Borders and Bridges*

lentlessness of his understanding of the church as under judgment. The church's constant tendency will be to manufacture defenses. In doing so, it will use all the right jargon, but it will be, as
he puts it, describing Job's comforters, like "cut flowers."[5] So it
must be that the word of judgment will often come from without.
If we fail to attend to the words without, we will squander the
opportunity for transformation, change, growth, renewal.
"What counts in the church," Barth says elsewhere, "is not
progress but reformation—its existence as *ecclesia semper reformanda*" (IV/1, 705).[6]

If we believe in semper reformanda (and how can we not, if
we have even a remotely decent account of sin?), we must engage those outside the walls of the church. Flannery O'Connor
once said that the reason her stories were so grotesque and
bizarre was that because "to the hard of hearing you shout, for
the almost blind you draw large and startling figures."[7] Barth
thinks the church is hard of hearing, and words from outside
may be the equivalent of the sort of shouting in which we might
have a chance at hearing the one Word.

This brings him to a second criterion for discerning such true
words: They lead us into a deeper engagement with Scripture.
That is, Barth simply assumes that we are not deeply enough engaged with Scripture. This is important because of the way it
seems to undermine his insistence that we test those words by
Scripture. But it doesn't undermine it. It clarifies it. It is not entirely clear to Barth that we are capable of performing this test,
since it is not clear to him that we read Scripture well. Again,
Barth breaks up the dichotomy the question presumed. But there
is a chance that our engagement with others will force us to read
Scripture well.

Yoder puts it like this:

> When the empirical community becomes disobedient,
> other people can hear the Bible's witness too. It is after all a
> public document. Loners and outsiders can hear it speak-
> ing, especially if the insiders have ceased to listen. It was
> thanks to the loner Tolstoy and the outsider Gandhi that the
> churchman Martin Luther King Jr. . . . was able to bring
> Jesus' word on violence back into the churches. It was
> partly the outsider Marx who has enabled liberation the-
> ologians to restate what the Law and Prophets had been

saying for centuries, largely unheard, about God's parti-sanship for the poor.[8]

So a space has opened up in which the believer is freed for an "absolute openness" to hear words of truth in this outer sphere.

But we have to be careful how we say this. Here one answer to the question about *how* we engage other words emerges. On the one hand, we have to be careful to not let those words crowd out the one Word. On the other hand, we have to be careful to listen patiently. I mean that the temptation will be to only hear those words that confirm what we already know. If that is all that happens, then it is the exact opposite of what Barth is trying to cultivate. It becomes just another way of shoring up our defenses. Edward Said identified this tendency as a hallmark of orientalist scholarship. "The East," he wrote, "is always *like* some aspect of the West."[9]

Perhaps at first glance this seems counter-intuitive. We think that colonialism operated by turning difference into radical difference that had to be subdued, repressed, and transformed by armies, embassies, missionaries, and cultural centers. That is certainly true. But Said is pointing out the other side of the colonial coin. He means that the Orientalists had an uncanny ability to not see difference when it suited them. If difference from us can be muted, then the challenge to us is equally muted. We turn the other into a confirmation of ourselves because we fear the transformation that would be demanded by a confrontation with difference.

This is what I earlier identified as the liberal view in discussions of interfaith dialogue, the idea that other religions are saying the same thing as Christianity, only in different, less adequate terms. It can sound like Barth is recommending something like this when he writes that "such words must be in the closest material and substantial conformity and agreement with the one Word" (111). Or when he writes that true words will be the words that provide "comfort and encouragement" to the church. But Barth quickly complicates this by adding, "It will be shown, however, that this is genuine comfort and encouragement, and not false temptation and enticement, by the fact that the community is not merely confirmed and approved by these words, but also shamed, frightened, unsettled, and corrected" (129).

[handwritten margin note: we might be too blind to recognize words that conform to the Word]

This in turn means that what counts as "closest material and substantial conformity and agreement with the one Word" is not knowable in advance. Barth is not saying that all we have to do is glance around and see what words are or are not reflecting the Word and then pay close patient attention to them. His whole point is that, given an awareness of our sinfulness, we will likely not be able to recognize, or will misrecognize, those words when we do see them. We have to pay close patient attention to discern which are or are not true words. What beautiful music might be playing that we are too tone-deaf to hear? How do we cultivate the kind of responsiveness, patience, and habits of listening that would enable us to hear?

The essays in this volume attest to various ways workers with Mennonite Central Committee have tried to cultivate such responsiveness and patience and have allowed themselves, MCC as an institution, and the Mennonite and Brethren in Christ churches more generally, to be pried open to new truths. They are too various to summarize easily, but the most frequently re-curring theme is relationships. In almost all of the essays in this volume, the authors highlight MCC's emphasis on long-term, personal relationships with partners and beneficiaries. MCC has usually insisted on long-term relationships with respect to development and peacemaking—these essays show that it is just as important for interfaith bridge building.

Although the emphasis on relationships can sometimes sound like a vague romanticism, in the Barthian terms I have employed so far, the demand for long-term relationships enacts a judgment. The aid worker, development worker, peacemaker, or bridge-builder is judged, a priori, as not just ignorant, but as presumptuous, arrogant, and apt to do more harm than good. Some of the larger aid and development agencies (most infamously, the various UN agencies) seem convinced that such weaknesses can be made up for by a vast, intricate, and mobile bureaucratic apparatus. MCC relies instead primarily on three-year personnel placements under the authority of local institutions. These volunteer placements don't always work. Projects carried out by local organizations with MCC financial support don't always work. And MCC struggles with the question of what it would mean to say that, for example, a particular peacebuilding (or interfaith bridge-building) project had "worked."[10]

Some in MCC are concerned that recent organizational developments—most notably, an emphasis on results-based management—push MCC several steps closer to the managerial rationality of the larger NGOs. It is characteristic of those agencies that

> humanitarian accountability declines in direct proportion to the relative power of the stakeholder. Humanitarian agencies are perceived to be good at accounting to official donors, fairly good at accounting to private donors and host governments, and very weak in accounting to beneficiaries.[11]

MCC's turn to results-based management means it is now much better at accounting to its donors. It remains to be seen if its traditional strength, accountability to beneficiaries made possible by the emphasis on relationships, is commensurately weakened.

At times, MCC worker placements and MCC-supported projects have produced surprising friendships and nurtured relationships that bridge faith divides, like the musical fellowship of the Pontanima choir, the friendship between Pak Paulus and Pak Agus, and community-based reconciliation between Christians and Muslims in Jos, Nigeria. The patience and commitment needed to forge and nurture these types of relationships, I would suggest, are the qualities we need to cultivate receptivity to what Barth calls the "parables of the kingdom" outside the walls of the church.

NOTES

1. Barry Lopez, *Arctic Dreams* (Toronto: Bantam, 1986), 109. Quoted in Coles, *Self/Power/Other: Political Theory and Dialogical Ethics* (Ithaca, NY: Cornell University Press, 1992), 1.

2. Coles, 2.

3. Karl Barth, *Church Dogmatics* IV/3, trans. G. W. Bromiley (Edinburgh: T & T Clark, 1961). All parenthetical page numbers in this chapter refer to this text.

4. Paul J. Griffiths, *Problems of Religious Diversity* (Oxford, England: Blackwell, 2001), 53.

5. It is of great importance that throughout IV/3, Barth repeatedly turns to the book of Job. The middle third of each book of volume four takes up human sinfulness. In the other volumes, Barth uses Christ as

the model of sinlessness illuminating the sinfulness of humanity. And in each section he uses various Old Testament figures to show our sin. But in IV/3, the model of sinlessness is Job, and the models of sinfulness are his comforters. That is, the model of sinlessness is an outsider (Job was not a Jew) and the models of sinfulness are consummate insiders.

6. Karl Barth, *Church Dogmatics* IV/1, trans. G. W. Bromiley (Edinburgh: T & T Clark, 1956(, 705.

7. "The Fiction Writer and His Country," in *Collected Works of Flannery O'Connor*, ed. Sally Fitzgerald (New York: Library of America, 1988), 805-6.

8. John Howard Yoder, *For the Nations* (Grand Rapids: Wm. B. Eerdmans, 1996), 93. In conversation following an MCC Peace Committee meeting, Iris de Leon Hartshorn of MCC US correctly reminded me that Yoder's characterization of Marx and Gandhi as "outsiders" is clumsy just insofar as it draws the lines between outside and inside too starkly. This is an important point, and it is only appropriate that it comes from Iris who, being from south Texas, is something of an expert on borderlands.

9. Edward Said, *Orientalism* (New York: Pantheon, 1978), 67.

10. More than one contributor to this volume has noted the question of whether or not the current emphasis within MCC on "results-based management," something that mirrors broader trends within secular and church organizations, fits well with the relationship-building that has characterized MCC's arguably most "successful" interfaith bridge-building projects.

11. Nicholas Stockton, "The Accountability Alibi." This paper as well as Stockton's "The Accountable Humanitarian" can be found at the website of the Humanitarian Accountability Partnership, www.hapinternational.org/en/.

Interfaith Bridge Building: MCC International Program Department "Key Initiative," 2006-2010

Bob Herr and Judy Zimmerman Herr
(prepared 2005)

1. WHAT IS A "KEY INITIATIVE"?

Key initiatives are MCC International Program Department areas of special focus for the five-year period of 2006 to 2010. Currently three are in place: work with HIV/AIDS, water, and interfaith bridge building. Key initiatives do not replace ongoing MCC country program work but are areas of special need and new program potential.

2. WHAT DO WE MEAN BY INTERFAITH BRIDGE BUILDING?

During the next five years, MCC's International Program

Department will look for new ways to work with non-Christian partners. This might include direct partnerships with agencies or organizations from other faiths. More often it will involve working with existing Christian partners as they establish partnerships across faith lines. An aim is to find ways to work together in service. In places where there is interfaith conflict, MCC may intentionally seek ways to work at peacebuilding between groups experiencing tension.

3. Is interfaith bridge building a faithful Christian witness?

Interfaith work begins with faith. For Christians, interfaith work means being clear about Christian convictions. This includes being centered on Jesus the Christ and on the central role of God's church on earth. Our confession is that Jesus Christ is Lord, that he is the way, truth, and life. Claiming that salvation comes through him need not inhibit forging alliances with those who do not share this conviction, nor should it prevent us from cultivating an ability to learn about God from those outside the Christian faith.

One temptation is to hold narrowly to an exclusive faith, unable to see God's work outside this narrow focus. Another is to shy away from particular convictions, to search for a neutral faith language. Both are weak convictions. On the one hand, there is no neutral ground to stand on, and on the other, God frequently challenges our understanding by speaking to us through the Other. We need to expect that people from different faiths will name the truths they discover in interfaith collaboration according to their own faith convictions. We, too, can engage in interfaith bridge building not from a low view of Jesus, seeing Jesus as only one light among many, but from a high view of Jesus. To deny that there is truth to be found outside the church, to deny the value of fostering friendships and collaboration among persons of different faiths, is to have too low a Christology.

Between Christians and Muslims, for example, commitment to God is the same. The focus of that commitment diverges, however. For Muslims, it is the Qur'an and the way of Muhammad. For Christians, the center is Jesus the Messiah. Both are committed to submission to the reign of God. The question is, "What is the nature of the reign of God?"

4. Why interfaith bridge building?

Many conflicts in our world today are identified as being between different faiths. Often religious identity is not the actual cause of the conflict but is one factor that is appealed to by parties to the conflict. This makes working at peacebuilding across religious fault lines especially important at this time.

5. How does MCC do this bridge building?

Working at peacebuilding across religious lines can take many forms, but MCC's particular gift is Christian service, working together to meet human need. It is logical, therefore, for MCC to work at interfaith bridge building in a "diaconal" way (i.e. from the basis of service). This includes finding ways to work together with people or agencies of other faiths at common service tasks, or supporting our church partners as they work at common tasks with partners of other faiths.

Who we work with will differ from place to place. A point of tension today is between Christianity and Islam. Thus MCC will look in many places for relationships with Islamic groups: in Central and South Asia, in the Middle East, and in Africa. In Latin America, where the divisions are between Catholic and Protestant or Evangelical churches, MCC works with that "interfaith" tension.

6. Projects that work with AIDS or with water are easier to understand in terms of what they are trying to accomplish, but what about interfaith bridge building? Can you describe the outcomes or impacts MCC expects from its interfaith bridge-building work?

Like much MCC peace work, interfaith bridge building is often a lens for approaching other work, rather than a result in itself. Development, health, or education work can be undertaken in partnership with a non-Christian agency or organization, to meet objectives in interfaith bridge building. The tasks at hand remain those related to specific needs, but the way of working at these needs may be via an interfaith partnership. While hard to quantify, we would look for improved relationships and understanding in a given location, or for greater openness across lines of conflict.

7. How is this different from interfaith dialogue? Or is it the same thing?

"Interfaith dialogue" usually refers to a discussion of theology or sacred texts, carried on by theologians or other specialists. This is generally not something MCC has expertise or background in and is not the focus of this initiative. In some cases in which relationships have developed over time, these may lead to interest in theological dialogue. An example is the MCC Iran program, through which supporting health clinics led to establishing student exchanges leading to a series of theological dialogues. MCC supports the dialogues, but they are largely directed by Toronto Mennonite Theological Centre. While in some cases our partnerships may lead to more theological interaction, or dialogue, our first aim with interfaith bridge building is building relationships by working together in response to human need.

8. What does interfaith bridge building mean for our Christian identity?

In relating to persons of other faiths, MCC programs and workers clearly identify themselves as Christians, to help partners understand what motivates our service. Often people of other faiths are less comfortable with secular than with faith identities and welcome interaction with people who express an explicit faith identity. In some cases clarity about our Christian identity may limit who is comfortable partnering with us.

9. Is MCC compromising its Christian identity by interaction with those of other faiths?

MCC works "in the name of Christ." Our work bears witness to the reign of Christ. This is our motivation and our confession. We seek to express our witness clearly and humbly, with the understanding that, just as we have a responsibility to offer what we have to others, God also has more to teach us. Working with and learning to know persons from other faiths can serve to strengthen our faith, in that we will be pushed to explain why we act and believe the way we do. As we build trusting relationships, we assume our conversation will include what is most important to us—our faith. This offers a chance to talk about what we have found as Christians, and to state what we believe. We look for respectful ways to do this.

10. Why use the metaphor of "bridge building?" Doesn't that imply a neutral meeting space, watering down our faith claims?

Building bridges is a common metaphor for peacemaking. There is often a divide, at least a perceived one, between followers of different religions. In many cases, this is an active conflict. The metaphor of a bridge implies that we seek to build a structure or channel for communication and interaction. The image is not meant to imply that we create some imagined, neutral space. MCC will continue to clearly identify itself as Christian and as motivated by our faith profession. We are not looking for neutral ground but for ways to interact, connect, build trust, and share tasks of service.

11. What will MCC do if it wants to work with a group from another faith but a Christian partner organization in the same location does not want us to?

MCC will listen to the counsel of current partners, especially Christian partners, when exploring opportunities for interfaith service. Counsel from a trusted partner saying that a new possibility is not wise will be taken seriously. All MCC programs have a system for seeking advice from local partners and advisors about work and partnerships, including especially Mennonite World Conference-related churches. We will rely on their counsel in exploring any new partnerships.

12. If we seek to partner with agencies of other faiths, isn't it possible that we will become partners of agencies who might seek to do harm—like terrorist groups? How will we know, since some groups can have multiple purposes?

MCC will rely on the counsel of trusted partners and friends when considering new partnerships. All programs that explore new ideas and possibilities, especially in contexts where trust is broken and conflict is a reality, contain some risk, and interfaith bridge building can never be free of risk. On occasion, MCC has worked with partners that we later discovered were not being completely truthful about their identity. This may happen again. Taking seriously the counsel of trusted local partners helps to guard against this happening.

13. If given the opportunity, will MCC engage in church planting via interfaith bridge-building activities?

The focus of this initiative is to work with and build trusting relationships with people from other faiths. If, in the course of this work and in response to the witness and testimony of MCC workers, friends are attracted to Christianity and want to start a church, MCC will walk alongside them. Based on experience, we expect this may happen. At the same time, we will be clear with partners that our aim is to work together in respectful and transparent ways for service. MCC does not have a hidden agenda.

Index

Catholic-Jewish-Muslim-
Orthodox-Protestant,
132-149
Christian-Hindu, 67, 72-84,
88-90, 150-159
Christian-Muslim, 17-30,
43-56, 92-93, 96-116, 132-
159, 173
Hindu-Buddhist, 71-74
Hindu-Muslim, 153-157
Mennonite-Catholic, 31-42,
103-104, 121, 132-149
Mennonite-Orthodox, 103-
104, 117-149
Mennonite-Protestant, 132-
149
Interreligious Center, Bel-
grade, Serbia, 137, 141-
144, 147-148
Iran, 105-116, 174
Iraq war, 12, 19, 64
Islam
in Indonesia, 22-27
in Nigeria, 46-48
in Somalia, 57-58
Islamic fundamentalism, *See*
Islamists
Islamists, 12, 114-115
in Egypt, 99
in Indonesia, 17-22, 28
in Palestine, 92-93
in Somalia, 60, 64
Israel-Palestine, *See* Palestine-
Israel

J
Jesus Christ
and doctrine, 65
and God's love and mercy,
152
and lordship, 161-165, 172,
174

and peace, 111, 134, 166
and salvation, 84, 102-103,
150-153, 161-165, 172
and service, 54, 56, 80, 84-
89, 130, 153
and unity, 117, 125-126
as model, 83, 123
centering in, following, 23,
26, 29
crossing borders, breaking
walls, 11-14, 33, 37-38,
112, 144-145, 150
sinlessness, 169-170
Jewish Center, Zagreb, Croatia,
137

K
Khatami, Muhammed, 105
Koran, *See* Qur'an
Kosovo, 141

L
Latin Patriarchate School of
Zababdeh, 94-98
Liberal Islam Network, 26, 28
Liberation theology, 96

M
Markovic, Ivo, 137-140, 143-
144, 148
Martens, Harry, 119-120
Martin, Ed, 108, 116, 122, 157
Martyrdom, Christian, 126
Mennonite Board of Missions
(MBM, now Mennonite
Mission Network, MMN),
66-69, 89-91, 123, 130
Mennonite Central Committee
(MCC), 12-14 and *passim*
Mennonite Middle East Refer-
ence Group (MMERG),
121-124

Shenk, Gerald, 134-136, 141,
143, 149
Somalia, 57-65
Southeast Europe, 132-149
Steele, David, 136-137, 149
Summer Peacebuilding Insti-
tute, Eastern Mennonite
University, 27, 125
Syria, 72, 99-100, 103, 112, 115-
131

T
Teachers Abroad Program
(TAP), MCC, 45
Toronto Mennonite Theologi-
cal Centre, University of
Toronto, 110, 116, 174
Trauma recovery, 20, 28, 44-46,
50-51

U
United Mission to Nepal
(UMN), 67-90
Statement of Values, 81-84

W
Wall, John, 138-139
Wall, Karin Kaufman, 138-139,
145-146
Wenger-Shenk, Sara, 135
World Hindu Federation
(WHF), 78

Y
Yoder, John Howard, 165-167,
170
Yugoslavia, former, *See* Southeast Europe

Z
Zakka I, Patriarch Ignatius,
Syrian Orthodox

Church, 117-118, 122,
125
Zionism, 95, 101-102
Zochrot Association, 95, 97-98

The Contributors

Susan Classen, Nerinx, Kentucky, is the director of Cedars of Peace, a small retreat center on the grounds of the Sisters of Loretto Motherhouse in central Kentucky. She worked with the Mennonite Central Committee (MCC) in Bolivia, El Salvador, and Nicaragua from 1981 to 2003. Susan's passion for peacemaking and for issues related to ecology grew out of her years in Latin America. She writes for a variety of publications and is the author of two books, *Vultures and Butterflies: Living the Contradictions* and *Dewdrops on Spiderwebs: Connections Made Visible*.

Peter Dula, Harrisonburg, Virginia, is Assistant Professor of Religion and Culture at Eastern Mennonite University. He has served Mennonite Central Committee (MCC) in Burundi, Jordan, and Iraq. He taught for one year at Meserete Kristos College in Ethiopia. He earned his Ph.D. in theology and ethics from Duke University in 2004 and has authored several academic articles.

Roy Hange, Charlottesville, Virginia, served under Mennonite Central Committee (MCC) in Egypt, Syria, and Iran for ten years. He is currently co-pastor with his wife Maren of Charlottesville Mennonite Church and is overseer of the Harrisonburg District of Virginia Mennonite Conference. He regularly writes and speaks on religious peacemaking.

Bob Herr and Judy Zimmerman Herr, Akron, Pennsylvania, are co-directors for Mennonite Central Committee's Program Development Department. They previously served as co-directors for MCC's International Peace Office and as administrators for MCC programs in South Africa. Together they edited *Transforming Violence: Linking Local and Global Peacemaking*.

Jeanne Zimmerly Jantzi, Indonesia, serves as Mennonite Central Committee Representative to Indonesia along with her husband, Daniel. They follow in the footsteps of her parents, who were also MCC workers in Indonesia. The family, which includes sons Ben, David, and Paul, previously served with MCC in Congo and Nigeria. Jeanne is a graduate of Eastern University with a master's degree in International Economic Development.

Chantal Logan, Harrisonburg, Virginia, was born in Paris, France. She earned a B.A. and an M.A. with a focus in linguistics from the University of Paris-Nanterre and a Ph.D. in comparative literature from the University of Limoges, France. Her other fields of study include psychotherapy, Islamic studies, and conflict resolution. She served with her husband under Eastern Mennonite Missions (EMM) and then in a joint appointment through EMM and Mennonite Central Committee (MCC) from 1995 to 2003 in East Africa, relating and working with Somali people. Presently, she teaches French, Spanish, and African literature at Eastern Mennonite University.

Edgar Metzler, Goshen, Indiana, did interdisciplinary studies as an undergraduate at Goshen College and graduate work in theology at Associated Mennonite Biblical Seminary, psychology at the University of Pittsburgh, and international relations at American University. He has worked in a variety of roles. In addition to serving as a pastor, he directed Peace Corps programs in Iran, Thailand, Nepal, and India. He worked as Executive Director of the United Mission to Nepal and in a variety of capacities with Mennonite Central Committee (MCC), most recently as its International Program director.

Randy Puljek-Shank, Sarajevo, Bosnia and Herzegovina, is the co-director of Mennonite Central Committee's program for Southeast Europe, together with his wife, Amela.

Jon Rudy, Mindanao, the Philippines, has been Mennonite Central Committee's Asia Peace Resource Person since 2001. Living in the Philippine Island of Mindanao, he has worked with MCC volunteers, partners, and programs throughout Asia on peace programs. He is a management committee member and facilitator at the annual Mindanao Peacebuilding Institute. A 2001 graduate of Eastern Mennonite Seminary and University, Rudy has worked with MCC since 1987 in Somalia, Swaziland, and Asia.

Gopar Tapkida, Jos, Nigeria, has served as the coordinator of Mennonite Central Committee peace work in Nigeria since

2001. He began the regional coordination of MCC peace work in West Africa in January 2007. Gopar currently leads multi-faith and inter-denominational peace and conflict transformation in Nigeria. He is the lead adjunct instructor in religious and identity-based conflict in three seminaries (ECWA Theological Seminary Jos, Apostolic Theological Seminary Jos, and Evengal Theological Seminary Jos) in Nigeria, and at the African Peace Institute at Mindolo, Zambia. He received his first degree in pastoral theology in Jos, Nigeria and a graduate degree in conflict analysis and transformation from Eastern Mennonite University, Harrisonburg, Virginia, USA. He is married to Monica and has three daughters.

Eldon Wagler and **Jane Emile-Wagler**, Partridge, Kansas, worked for Mennonite Central Committee in Egypt and Syria from the early 1990s until 2007, most recently as Country Representatives for Syria. They have two children, Anthony and Mary.

Alain Epp Weaver, Chicago, Illinois, worked in a variety of capacities with the Middle East program of Mennonite Central Committee for eleven years, most recently as co-representative for Palestine, Jordan, and Iraq. Among other edited and authored books, he is the editor of *Under Vine and Fig Tree: Biblical Theologies of Land and the Palestinian-Israeli Conflict* (Cascadia 2007) and the author of numerous articles, both academic and popular.

Lightning Source UK Ltd.
Milton Keynes UK
UKOW051024200812

197778UK00001B/177/A